Build up, Build up, Prepare the Road!

The Life of Miss Thomasine Allen

Yasuko Meguro

Kyo Bun Kwan

Build up, Build up, Prepare the Road!
© 2015 Yasuko Meguro

All rights reserved. No part of this publication may be reproduced or transmitted in any form or by any means, electronic or mechanical, including photocopy, recording, or any information storage and retrieval system, without permission in writing from the author and publisher.

Publisher:
KYO BUN KWAN Inc. (Christian Literature Society of Japan)
4-5-1 Ginza, Chuo-ku, Tokyo, 104-0061, JAPAN.
Tel: +81-3-3561-5549
Fax: +81-3-5250-5107
URL: http://www.kyobunkwan.co.jp/publishing/

Cover design: Hiroto Kumagai

Printed in Japan.
ISBN 978-4-7642-9964-1

Thomasine Allen (1890-1976)

Dwell deep, my soul, dwell deep! I am not my body, my body is only the physical house in which I live. The essential thing about me is my spiritual life. So long as I am honest and true and trust in God, my soul is beyond the reach of all adversity. No No trouble can touch the essential and eternal 'me'. Because I am God's child I can meet all that comes in the day's work bravely and serenely.

Thomson Allen.

"DWELL DEEP": Autograph poem by Miss Allen (See p. 40)

Thomas Allen,
Thomasine's father

Lola Allen,
Thomasine's mother

Miss Allen in a kimono,
1915

Miss Allen, 1911

Class of 1919, Shokei Girls School in Sendai:
Miss Buzzell (sixth right, front) and Miss Allen (sixth left, front)
(See p. 29)

Anti-prostitution organization in Morioka:
Miss Allen (center, front) and Kuni Obara (fifth left, front)
(See p. 42)

Boys' club in Morioka

Sunday school in Morioka

Miss Allen wearing waraji
(See p. 46)

A lone pine tree in Takata-Matsubara
that survived the Tsunami of 2011

Summer School of four hundred children
(See p. 46, 58)

William Merrell Vories
(See p. 70, 111)

Miss Allen in Kuji,
1938

Temma Nobechi visits Kuji, 1940
(See p. 69)

Children in Kuji kindergarten
(See p. 68)

The Schroers
(See p. 84, 95)

Miss Allen comes back to Japan in 1947
(See p. 115)

Tule Lake Relocation Center
(See p. 105)

The Farmer's Gospel School: Takeshi Yahaba (far left, back)
(See p. 132)

New station wagon
(See p. 150, 152)

Citation Ceremony of the Association for Japan-U.S. Amity and Trade Centennial on November 10, 1960: Mrs. McKenzie (left)
(See p. 209)

Mr. & Mrs. Reischauer visit Miss Allen;
At Homare Elementary School
(See p. 224)

Miss Allen's 50th Anniversary
of Work in Japan
(See p. 226)

Miss Allen received The Fourth Order of the Sacred Treasure:
Miss Allen (fourth right, front)
(See p. 231)

Teaching at Allen Junior College

Miss Allen with her students

Funeral service held at Kuji Kindergarten
(See p. 258)

Civic funeral service held by the Kuji city

Chronological Table

Biographical Timeline of Miss Allen		Timeline of Japanese History
	1868	Meiji Restoration
	1874	Freedom and People's Rights Movement supported
		The government hires foreign employees as teachers, technicians and advisers
	1880	Freedom and People's Rights Movement supported
	1885	First group emigrants to Hawaii
	1889	Promulgation of the Meiji Constitution
1890 Born at Franklin County, Indiana in U.S.A. (Sept. 30)	1890	First General Election: First Session of the Imperial Diet
	1894 -95	Sino-Japanese War
	1902	Anglo-Japanese Alliance
	1904 -05	Russo-Japanese war
1908 Begins attending Franklin College of Indiana	1910	Annexation of Korea
1911 Becomes a teacher in Albemarle, North Carolina	1911	Factory Law of 1911 enacted to protect laborers
1912 Learns and prepares for mission service in Biblical Seminary in New York; Works in a New York settlement house of the American Parish of the Presbyterian Church	1912 -26	Taisho Period
1914 WABFMS appoints her as principal of Sarah Curtis Home in Tokyo	1914 -19	Japan enters the First World War
1915 Lands in Yokohama port on the *Mongolia* (Sept. 10)		
1917 Transfers to Shoukei Girl's School in Sendai (Miyagi Pref.)	1918	Rice riots of 1918, provoked by spiraling inflation
1921 Establishes Shin-ei Kindergarten in Taira (Fukushima Pref.)	1920	The first celebration of May day in Japan
1922 Establishes Seiko Kindergarten in Shiogama (near Sendai); Meets Dr. Inazo Nitobe and Dr. Toyohiko Kagawa	1923	Great Kanto Earthquake
	1926 -89	Showa Period
1927 Returns to the U.S. and enrolls in the graduate school of the University of Chicago	1927	Financial Crisis of 1927
1929 After earning a master's degree, returns Morioka to start community evangelism in Iwate Pref.	1930 -31	Showa depression
Director of Uchimaru Kindergarten in Morioka; Establishes Morioka Shinjo Christian Center	1931	Poor harvest by cold weather damage

		1932	The establishment of Manchukuo
1929 -38	Relief operation for serious cold-weather damage and Great Tsunami	1933	Great earthquake in Tohoku
1938	Moves to Kuji; Establishes Kuji Christian Center and Kuji Kindergarten	1939	National Service Draft Ordinance for strategies industries
1941	Apprehended at her house in Kuji	1941	Pacific War begins: Japanese attack Pearl Harbor
1941 -43	Internment Camp in Morioka, Sendai and Tokyo		
1943	Arrives at New York Port on the *Gripsholm* (Nov. 29)		
1943 -47	Works at the War Relocation Center for Japanese-Americans	1945	Atomic bomb drops on Hiroshima and Nagasaki; Japan accepts the Potsdam Declaration; Instrument of Surrender signed aboard the USS Missouri
1947	Comes back to Japan, Restarts "God's work" in Kuji; Establishes Farmer's Gospel School and Kuji Center Clinic	1946	Promulgation the Constitution of Japan
1948	Establishes Homare Educational Foundation	1951	San Francisco Peace Treaty and U.S.-Japan Security Treaty signed
1952 -58	Establishes Homare Elementary Schoool, Seikei Dressmaking School, Homare Junior High School, Dairy-Farming Center and Christian Dairy Farming School	1956	Soviet-Japanese Joint Declaration; Japan granted membership in the United Nations
1958	Awarded The Fifth Order of the Sacred Treasure; Testimonial of her work of social welfare from Japan; Retirement from Missionary work; Decides to stay on in Kuji		
1959	Receives Honorary Degree of Doctor of Humane Letters from Franklin College (Jul. 8); Becomes Honorary citizen of Kuji City (Nov. 3)	1959	Declaration of a sister city relationship between Kuji City and Franklin City
1960	Relief Activity for Great Sanriku huge Tsunami; Invited to the Association for Japan-U.S. Amity and Trade Centennial	1960	Second of the U.S.-Japan Security Treaty signed; Chilean Tsunami
1964	Women's clubs of the churches in the U.S. establish Kuji Christian Center Foundation; Elizabeth Anne Hemphill publishes "A Treasure To Share"	1964	Tokyo Olympic Games
1965	Receives a visit from Dr. & Mrs. Reischauer (Sep. 19); Miss Allen's 50th Anniversary of work in Japan by Kuji city (Oct. 4)	1965	Japan Congress against Atomic and Hydrogen Bombs
1968	Awarded the Fourth Order of the Sacred Treasure (Oct. 23)		
1970	Homare Educational Foundation is authorized in the U.S.; Establishes Allen Junior College	1970	EXPO '70 opens in Osaka
1976	Dies on Jun. 7	1976	Lockheed Scandal

Map

And it will be said:
"Build up, build up, prepare the road!
Remove the obstacles out of the way of my people."
(Isaiah 57:14, NIV)

Contents

FOREWORD	7
PREFACE	9

I. "Sunshine in the Soul" — 13

1. Father's Will	14
2. Salah Curtis Home in Tokyo	22
[Report 1] Reaches Japan and is Given Hearty Welcome by School	22
[Poem 1] *HE KNOWETH*	27
3. Northern Castle Town—Sendai	29

II. "To Sow the Seeds, To Try to Follow up on Results" — 39

[Poem 2] *DWELL DEEP*	40
1. "Go where the need is greatest": Morioka (1929–38)	41
[Report 2] Christmas in July	45
2. Damage from Cold Weather and the Great Tsunami (1931–34)	48
3. The Layman's Missionary Inquiry (1932–38)	55
[Document 1] Letter from Dr. Charles P. Emerson (1932)	56
[Report 3] In Pine Grove and Temple Grounds	58
4. My Home Town—Kuji	63
[Report 4] The Baptist Observer, Dec. 2, 1937	65
[Report 5] We Have Built	71
[Document 2] Letter from Bishop Norman Binsted (1940)	75

III. World War II (1941–43) — 79

1. The Outbreak of War: Detention — 81

[Report 6] Letter from Internment Camp — 87

2. "We are free here, and we can talk." — 89

[Report 7] New York, Dec. 9, 1943 — 94

[Document 3] *I DON'T DESERVE THAT MEDAL* — 101

IV. After the War (1947–) — 113

1. Go Back to My Home Town — 115

[Report 8] A Country Trip — 117

[Report 9] Friendship Day and Days — 120

[Note 1] Kuji Kindergarten — 126

2. To Build and To Plant (1948–49) — 130

[Report 10] Nearer Our Goal — 137

[Report 11] Kuji Christian Center 1948-1949 — 141

[Report 12] Kuji Christmas 1949 — 146

[Report 13] The Year's Blessings, Kuji Christian Center 1949-1950 — 148

[Report 14] Wagon Wheels — 152

3. "Training the Mind, Education" — 155

[Note 2] Some Thoughts on Education — 155

[Report 15] memo — 158

[Report 16] The Baggage and I — 161

[Report 17] Christmas Wholesale — 164

[Document 4] Letter from Japan Heifer Advisory Comittee (1955) — 172

[Document 5] Letter from Japan Heifer Advisory Comittee (1956) — 173

[Document 6] Letter from Sunshine Farm Dairy (1957) — 175

[Document 7] Letter from Mr. A. W. Huston to Mr. G. Leach (1958) — 176

[Report 18] memo	178
[Document 8] Greeting by Dr. Toyohiko Kagawa (1958)	179
[Report 19] Seedtime and Harvest	180
[Poem 3] *LIVING IN JOYFUL EXPECTATION*	185
[Report 20] Christmas in 1958	187
4. Retirement From Missionary Work and Honorary Awards	**190**
[Document 9] Letter from Franklin College	192
[Document 10] Letter from Franklin College (Apr. 1959)	194
[Document 11] Letter from Franklin College (Jul. 1959)	196
[Document 12] Kuji Mayor's congratulatory Speech (Nov. 1959)	197

V. "The Way to Better Tomorrow"	**201**
1. Relief Activity	**203**
[Report 21] After the Tidal Wave	204
2. "I Have a Great Treasure that I Want to Share."	**209**
[Report 22] memo	213
[Report 23] Again the Two Trees	215
3. Supporters: She Made Kuji Her Permanent Home	**220**
[Document 13] Kuji Christian Center Foundation	221
[Document 14] Paper by Mrs. Hemphil (Bitty)	221
[Document 15] Foreword of *A Treasure to Share*	223
[Document 16] Letter from Dr. E. O. Reischauer (1964)	224
[Document 17] Letter from Mrs. Haru Reischauer (1964)	225
[Document 18] Letter from Dr. E. O. Reischauer (1965)	226
[Document 19] Letter from Mrs. Maki Vories Hitotsuyanagi (1965)	227
[Report 24] The Dialogue on a Hillside	228
[Report 25] memo	231

6 | *Contents*

[Document 20] Congratulatory Speech by the Minister of Education 233

[Document 21] Letter from Mrs. Haru Reischauer (1969) 235

[Report 26] The Little Tree Presents Her Problem 237

4. Allen Junior College: Department of English Language and

English Literature 242

[Report 27] Our New Junior College 242

[Note 3] The Opening Address of Allen Junior College 244

[Note 4] Educational Principles 245

[Report 28] The Two Trees again Walk and Talk 247

VI. "Dwell Deep" 251

1. In Her Later Years 252

[Report 29] The Little Tree Is Happy 253

[Report 30] The Little Tree Is Cold 254

2. On Her Deathbed 257

BIBLIOGRAPHY 261

AFTERWORD 263

Foreword

Hiroki FUNAMOTO

(Professor Emeritus; Kwansei Gakuin University,
Ex-President; Tokyo Woman's Christian University)

Thomasine Allen is an American woman missionary who came to Japan in 1915 (Taisho 4) when she was only 25. At the beginning she taught in the kindergartens and girls' high schools in both Tokyo and Sendai; but after meeting with Nitobe Inazo and Kagawa Toyohiko, she was given the chances of mission in Japanese farms and villages.

However, after she moved to Iwate influenced by the thought of their Christianity, she gave her love to those who needed help.

Allen's motto is "to work with people with her best possible power, when it is needed."

It was when she was 80, she established Allen International Junior College in Kuji, Iwate. But unfortunately she fell in February 1976 when it was cold and broke her thighbone and was taken to the hospital, which led her to a most tragic end on the 7th of June. When her funeral was held, there was a big curtain "Honorary Citizen of Kuji, Thomasine Allen Sensei".

Meguro's book is entitled "Michinoku no Michi no

Saki—Thomasine Allen no Shogai", English title "Build up, Build up, Prepare the Road!—The Life of Thomasine Allen." It consists of 13 chapters in 293 pages with detailed notes of 196.

This book is not what praises what Allen did, but it looks into the historical references faithfully with a cool analytical mind, and tries to make out what she did; it was full of suggestions given to Japanese people with sharp eyes.

In March 11, 2011, the big earthquake disaster brought very big tragedies to Japan, but at the same time it brought very deep questions of what Japanese people should think about their own country.

This happening just overlaps with Sanriku Tsunami (a seismic sea wave at Sanriku) which Allen experienced herself twice at the beginning of the Showa Period (March 3, 1933; May 24, 1960) and her devoted life there is now vividly presented before us.

In this sense, I think the book is published quite timely when it should be.

Preface

"Why art thou in Kuji? I always answer like this;
I must share a gift that God gave me."
(Waka SHIMOKOU, "Gunryoku" vol. 14 no. 4,
Tokyo, 2002, p. 26)

When I had completed the manuscript of this book, on March 11, 2011, the Great East Japan Earthquake occurred. It was the same gruesome scenery of the Tsunami that Miss Allen had seen twice on the same coast-land in Tohoku. In 1933, the terrible scene made her determined to move to Kuji; a very isolated and inconvenient rural town in Iwate Prefecture. In the early Showa period, people's life in the northern areas was miserable, suffered from cold-weather, poor harvest and earthquake-tsunami.

Before preaching on "Christ's love" and "Graced Soul", she tried to integrate herself into the rural life in poverty and exerted herself to make the people's life happier and richer. She had a strong desire to show "Joy to live" and "Pleasure to work" to the people. It was the mission for Miss Allen. She devoted herself to the spreading of her fundamental principle; "Happy life by helping each other". Her missionary activities were expended to work for bringing a better life; education, medical care, social welfare, dairy farming, and to make the local society active and happy.

As Miss Allen was well versed in Japanese religion, folklore and lifestyles, her missionary work reached into the Japanese people's hearts naturally. In the early Showa period, people's life, particularly in northern Iwate, was miserable. They suffered from cold-weather, poor harvest, tsunamis, etc. Miss Allen's work extended to activities helping the people of whole areas in Iwate. Such activities were supported by her many friends, not only in Japan but in the United States, by fundraising and by sending relief goods. The expenditure for her work was constantly exceeding her income as a missionary. To cope with the increased financial costs, she wrote many letters to her friends (almost every day!) reporting her activities, expressing her gratitude, asking for their help. (Her typewriter is now setting in the corner of the small kitchen of her house in Kuji.) In 1932, some of the letters were compiled into reports which met with a strong public response in the U.S. when it appeared in American magazines and newspapers.

Several years ago, in the Allen's house in Kuji I had found a lot of files in her study room. There were a lot of papers which she had written, many bundles of letters to her, several recording tapes and the transcriptions of an oral history tape interview of Thomasine Allen in *A Treasure to Share* written by Mrs. Elizabeth Hemphill. On Allen's words from the transcriptions I marked the (*) and added page number at the end

Preface

of sentences. I have to say that I would not have been able to write this book unless such relics had not existed. I composed Miss Allen's life in chronological order using such literature. There are some sentences which have been written, but I hope the reader will be patient to read theses sentences as I am sure he/she will come to appreciate her brilliant and meaningful words.

Yasuko MEGURO

Explanatory Note

Sentences marked with a mark " * " are Miss Allen's words, taped by Mrs. Hemphil and by NHK (Japan Broadcasting Corporation). I quoted them from her book *A Treasure to Share* and the tape.

Reference Data

1 **[Report 1]-[Report 30]**

   Copies of letters written by Miss Allen from 1915 through 1974.

2 **[Poem 1]-[Poem 3], [Note 1]-[Note 4]**

   Copies of Poems and Essays written by Miss Allen.

3 **[Document 1]-[Document 21]**

   Copies of letters to Miss Allen from her friends and all concerned.

I

"Sunshine in the Soul"

CHAPTER I

Father's Will

* "Many people, both American and Japanese, ask me why
on earth I ever came to an isolated place in Japan like Kuji.
And I tell them the reason: I have a very great treasure that
I want to share." (A. Hem., p. 14)

Miss Allen's father, Thomas Allen had passed away
shortly before she was born. Facing death he said to her
mother Lola. "Please educate my new born baby as a worker
for Jesus." Lola Wagoner Allen, a devoted Christian, named
her Thomasine after her father's name and decided to make a
good home for her two daughters, Thomasine and Margaret.
Lola bought the premises next to the Franklin College and
rented some rooms to young college girls. Every morning
small children had to recite verses from the Bible and every
evening they held family worship. Lola forced them to practice
the piano, saying: "After you've grown up, you will understand
the reason why I did it." She would want to give them the

I. "Sunshine in the Soul" | 15

most excellent culture from all over the world with the grace of her faith and love for Jesus.

Thomasine Allen was born in Franklin, Indiana, on 30th September, 1890. Her father Thomas Allen had died of typhoid fever. On his deathbed he asked his wife Lola to take good care of their children, developing missionary's ability. According to their last promise, Lola had brought up daughters very strictly.

But what was in Franklin that awakened a little girl's interest to be a missionary of a far-off poverty-stricken rural country in Japan; what was there? Franklin was not a large town, but a quiet and pious environment for cultivating young minds. Franklin College was closely relating to the First Baptist Church. The two institutions were so closely connected as to be almost intertwined, and in the realms of ethics and morals, their teaching dovetailed. Students worshiped and studied in a remarkably consistent atmosphere provided by the church and college helped to influence in her life of mission.

Lycurgus Waggoner (Lola's father) was serving as a deacon of Franklin First Baptist Church, and always stood with the faction which emphasized the importance of education. In those days when Miss Allen was born, the community, the college and the Church were sharing responsibility for training the young people of the town. About forty years later, we can see his influence reviving in Allen's projects of the foundation of education facilities; kindergarten, elementary school, and a new college in small rural town in Japan.

BUILD UP, BUILD UP, PREPARE THE ROAD!

During the time Miss Allen had been a college student, from 1908 to 1911, the Student Volunteer Movement was a strong current in the United States. In Franklin the Student Volunteers had regular meetings for prayer and consultation. Outside the College, speakers appealed for the needs of foreign mission and to become a member.

> * In the day the Student Volunteer Movement was very strong and largely under the leadership of John R. Motto, Sherwood Eddy, and Robert E. Spear. The slogan was "Evangelize the world in this generation," We believed that if we all did our duty as we saw it, we could evangelize the world. It was a great motto. The fact that it was too big what we could do was another matter; at least our ideals were up there. (A. Hem., p. 21)

Miss Allen could understand the impact of a phenomenal collegiate movement, but she was enjoying her college activity; YMCA and Pi Beta Phi. Naturally cheerful and sociable, she could delight her friends with her sense of humor. She thought that a good missionary was made not born.

> * I loved dancing and card playing, but I noticed that it bothered my mother and also some of the professors. They felt distressed about it and thought I ought to be more of an example, that if I was going to be a foreign missionary I ought not to do these things. Of course this was part of the times in 1910. Christian sentiment at that time was opposed to things like that and in favor of a very strict observance

of the Sabbath. After a great deal of thought and prayer, I decided that I would give up dancing and cards. It was hard—one of the hardest things I think I ever had to do, but at least it showed me that I could give something up and at the same time be happy. (A. Hem., p. 21)

After graduating from college in 1911, she got a job as a teacher in Albemarle, North Carolina. The next year she moved to New York and enrolled at the Biblical Seminary. At the same time, she worked in a New York Settlement house which was part of the American Parish of the Presbyterian Church. Under the leadership of Dr. Norman Thomas, the settlement house was a house for the many new immigrants of the Upper Eastside, who came from Italy, Hungary, and other eastern European nations. To put it short, it was a world of violence. "Don't you walk out alone at night, Miss Allen, any time, any place we'll go with you." Two Italian boys came forward as guardians. And they told their experience.

* You know what frisking is, don't you? We used to hold up people, and I would frisk the pockets and somebody else would hold the gun. One night in December I frisked a man's pockets and found ten dollars. The man said, "Oh, I was saving that money to buy Christmas presents for my children." I felt sorry about that, and I made the gang give the money back to him. I told them I would take them some- place else. We went to another end of the park and held up another man and got one hundred dollars. "Now then, I told

the gang," I told you it paid to do right!" (A. Hem., p. 22)

In this settlement there was not only fighting, violence, guns or knives, but Boy Scout troops, Camp Fire Girls, Bible study, and clubs or meetings for adults.

> * It was a neighborhood house in every sense of the word. Work in the family and in the community was another stepping-stone and a great help in preparation for the mission field. When I got to Japan it was invaluable to know that missionary work was more than just teaching the Bible and working in a church that was already organized. What good is your religion if it doesn't change lives? (A. Hem., p. 23)

After three years' seminary training, Miss Allen could gain confidence for becoming a foreign missionary. She made contact with the Woman's American Baptist Foreign Mission Society (WABFMS).

> * I didn't care what field, and I didn't even particularly care whether it was the foreign field or not. I was quite happy in the work among foreigner in the New York City settlement. I knew that there were many people who were more earnest Christians than I by far, but who could not go to the foreign field for various reasons. There was no reason why I could not go, and I felt that I must go where the need is greatest. I felt strongly even then, and this has been the guiding element in my life. (A. Hem., p. 23)

I. "Sunshine in the Soul" | 19

In a while, she was appointed to be the principle of the Sarah Curtis Home, a Girls' High School in Tokyo, Japan.

> * Going to Japan in that day and generation was quite different from going any place today when the whole world has become one. One time I asked what kind of house I could expect to live in, and I was told that would be an ordinary Japanese house. Of course, that didn't mean a thing to me because I had no idea what a Japanese house was like! Now people are so much better prepared for such a change in living, but then it was just a great big adventure, and we had no idea what we were facing. (A. Hem, p. 237)

[The American Women Missionaries and Education of Japanese Women]

Japanese people had a fixed idea about gender equality in America. They thought that it was well established in the States compared with other countries, especially with Japan. But it was only in 1920 that women's suffrage was finally authorized by law in the US. American wives helped their husbands who had all rights and responsibilities in their homes. Exemplary women were supposed to keep a comfortable home and bring-up children. In those days, the gender equality was regarded only as a principle and men did not care much about it.

At that time, roughly speaking, there were not many occupations available for women, other than teaching jobs or missionary work. Although even many women missionaries could not have the same authority and responsibility as the men had. And they were not allowed to baptize, to translate the Bible, to teach theology, or to establish churches. In 1859 when a woman missionary came to Japan, she was a wife of a male missionary.

In 1870, the Women's American Baptist Foreign Mission Society was established in America. Finally, women's liberationists were the Christians in mission work. Riding on the large tide of sending missionaries to Asia, many women missionaries crossed over the Pacific Ocean and went to Asian countries. As stated above, women missionaries' activity was very limited at that time and they gathered housewives, children and young people in the community and opened mother's clubs, day nurseries, bible classes, English classes etc.

In 1612, Japan closed the country to foreigners, and therefore for more than 250 years, Japan didn't go to war with any foreign countries and there were no domestic battles. In those peaceful days, Japanese culture matured in every field. Certainly during that period Japan had been a feudal society which had four social classes; warriors, farmers, craftsmen, and merchants. Each of the feudal lords founded "*Hanko*" which was an educational institution for their children and also their vassal's children. Gradually those schools were opened to many children and young people from the middle or the lower classes.

The curriculum of the school *Hanko* was expanded from the teaching of Confucian studies to classical Japanese studies, medicine, mathematics, chemistry, astronomy, military studies etc. The children entered at age 6 or 7 and completed their course between the ages of 15 or 20. By 1860, there were about 255 *Hanko* nationwide. In provincial areas, there was another educational system "*Terakoya*" that was similar to *Hanko*, but it was private, and opened to girls too. So from the 17th century Japan kept a highly literate level in the world.

After the Meiji Restoration, the new Japanese government attached more importance to school education and hastened to make up the modern education system for children and young people with the intention to teach them western knowledge, and advanced studies. In 1885 education for six years was made compulsory. But on the other hand, much attention was not paid to girls and children in those times. The government favorably received the women missionary activities to establish girls' high schools and kindergartens everywhere they wanted. Already, the first girls' school was founded in 1870 in Yokohama by Miss Mary E. Kidder, who was the first woman missionary to come to Japan.

"By 1889, thirty four girls' schools were established throughout Japan." #8 (Kobi., p. 185)

The girls of these missionary schools were eager to learn western knowledge, Christianity, English, and western culture. After they had graduated from school, some of them became excellent assistants of missionaries or married Japanese pastors. Many girls introduced the spirit of Christianity and modern lifestyle into Japanese ordinary life. It is sure that they and their children helped to speed up the construction of a new Japan and to promote Christian love in the 20th century. It was the time when Japanese people began to think about liberty, equality and charity. Thus the American Women Missionaries made a great and wide contribution to Japanese modernization after the Meiji Restoration wide.

CHAPTER 2

Salah Curtis Home in Tokyo

In 1915, Miss Allen was twenty-five years old when she went aboard on the *Mongolia* for Japan. On the passenger boat, she met 250 missionaries and their families who were going to the Orient. They had talked and discussed about facing an unknown future with beating hearts and uneasy feeling. They were liable to be depressed by those monotonous days. Miss Allen naturally was very witty, talked about something amusing with them and sung hymns on her piano. She made many friends who would be her supporters for her later projects in Tohoku, northern Japan. The Mongolia came into the Yokohama harbor on 10th September, 1915.

[Report 1]
 Reaches Japan and is Given Hearty Welcome by School
 Tokyo, Japan, Sept. 14, 1915

Dearest Home Folks:
 There is so much to tell I hardly know where to begin.

I am so sleepy and tired I'm afraid I won't get it straight anyway. But I want this to catch the boat tomorrow.

You know the "Mongolia" couldn't go into harbor so little canoes took us to shore at Yokohama and brought our friends out to meet us. Miss Carpenter, who is associated with Miss Whiteman met me. Also Dr. Dearing and Mr. Grassed. Dr. Dearing saw about our luggage and took it through the customs for us. Then Miss Carpenter, who is such a jolly person, Miss Pauley and I got into rikisha and was taken to Mrs. McArthur's. She is a daughter of Mrs. Ashore. Her husband was a very prosperous businessman and her home is an oriental dream. We were warned that it was not a missionary home so that we would not expect to live so handsomely. We arrived there about four o'clock Sunday afternoon and were almost immediately served tea, with a most elegant tea service, beautiful china, daintily arranged flowers, delicious sandwiches, hot biscuits, jam and ginger. There is scarcely an American thing in the whole house. At about eight o'clock we had dinner and during that two people whom I had known at the bible school in New York called as they lived just next door.

The house is located on a bluff and the view, with the city all brilliantly lighted, was most picturesque. The front of the house is the back. I mean the garden and entrance are not on the street. That night I had my first Japanese bath, and it was most interesting. There is a large deep wall tub filled with water and a pipe running up from one side. A fire is made inside of the tub and water is heated that way. Then there is a little tub shallow but longer than our foot tubs and water is dipped into this and you soap yourself, then rinse off in the large tub. Before retiring Mrs. McArthur gave us each a beautiful drawn work handkerchief. Next morning the dear little Japanese maid came in and arranged all of our clothes in neat piles and even got our stockings ready to put on and got the bath ready.

After breakfast we called jinrikisha and were taken to the Consulate to register. There we had to sign about five papers, swearing allegiance, etc. Then we went to the bank and got all of our money changed into yen and sen (Japanese money), and took a train for Tokyo. The station in Tokyo looks quite like the one in New York and is just a new one. The people are so tiny and the houses look quite like doll houses. I'm about twice too tall. I took a rikisha up to the school. It seems quite inhuman to be pulled by one of those tiny little men.

I was most pleasantly surprised to find such a beautiful place (am sending you a picture of it). There is a beautiful garden in front. The house is circular, half Japanese and half foreign, but they are joined together. Miss Whitman met me at the door and gave me a very hearty welcome. She is a dear, and all the girls ware there too and bowed and bowed. All seemed so happy to see me. They are so cute and sweet. My room is a large front one with four windows and a big closet. My trunks were delivered immediately so I unpacked and placed things in order.

This invitation was brought up to me. Also the program I am enclosing. The party was this afternoon and was a brilliant success. They first had a solemn welcome service. Two girls welcomed me in English, hoping I would stay forever. Then the welcome song by the school:

I. "Sunshine in the Soul" | 25

"To our teacher who has just come"
In this school where the flowers blossom and
    the birds are singing,
After receiving your instruction
    we shall strive to be diligent,
Holding on your sleeves.

To our teacher whom we welcome today
Though we are like cherry trees
    we shall bathe in the dew
Of thy blessings till we,
    growing stronger and stronger,
Shall become pillars in the Kingdom of God.

Then the 100th Psalm was read and prayer offered. Then I was presented with a beautiful bouquet of flowers. After that they said they would have a Japanese entertainment and we could laugh all we wanted to. They had some funny dialogues. (Miss Whitman explained them to me.) We had Koto and Samisen music and beautiful tableaux. Japanese tea was then served with little cakes.

The Language school opens next week. I am so glad we have a few days first for it is still very oppressive.

I am most pleasantly situated and am going to love it here I know. I have not told you near all. Sorry I can't write more, and write to more people, but tell them about it, as I cannot possibly write to all now. It's been rather strenuous living.

26 | BUILD UP, BUILD UP, PREPARE THE ROAD!

I love you all dearly, lovingly.
Thomasine Allen

For the first two years, Miss Allen lived at the school house with students, studying at the Japanese language school. Her work with students was limited to ordinary contacts, but she could have pleasant times to practice languages each others and to enjoy recreation for the girls.

* We had lots of fun in language school, for all of us were grown people who had had some experience in life; yet we were all just little kindergarten children learning to say, "What is this? It is a book. It is a clock."

We had good time there as we kept all of the American holidays, all of the British holidays, and all of the Japanese holidays, In the meantime, we studied Japanese. Of course I went to the Japanese church, and I often played the organ at some of the services. On one of the first Sundays I heard the pastor repeating my name all through his sermon. In Japanese, "Thomasine" is pronounced "tamasi-i", which means "soul". Japanese pastors used "tamashi-i" in their every other sentence. I wondered how on earth he knew my name, and why he was talking about me. Finally, I asked her, "Why are they talking about me? They don't know me! What is that word?" She explained that tamashi-i is the word that means soul, and of course, it was quite right and proper that the pastor should be talking about the soul! Other missionaries had had such problems, too.

Miss Jessie, with whom I live in Sendai, was quite disturbed one Sunday because pastors were insisting that even cats can be saved. Actually he was talking about "Nicodemus", but "Nicodemus" pronounced in Japanese is "nekodemo" which means "even cats". Miss Jessie was sure there was something wrong with the pastor's theology since he kept saying that even cats can be saved! (A. Hem., p. 28)

After a while, she was beginning to think about the missionary's duty and also to realize that the many kinds of problems of Japanese churches were very serious and quite vexing. Her efforts were rewarded and she could pass the last language examinations and take up her duties. The Mission was feeling the pinch of finances so the Salah Curtis Home (the Surugadai Girls School) had to be closed. She was transferred to Shokei Girls School in Sendai, north of Tokyo.

[Poem 1]

SEPTEMBER 30 SUNDAY.
Thomasine Allen, Tokyo, Japan

For God's richest endurance of power on this young missionary.

"Give us clear vision to see and strength to do the will of God." (John 8:31)

HE KNOWETH

The twilight falls, the night is near;
    I hold my work away,
And kneel to one who bends to hear

The story of the day.

The old, old story; yet I kneel
      To tell it at Thy call;
And cares grow lighter as I feel
      My Father knows them all.

Yes, all! The morning and the night,
      The joy, the grief, the loss,
The roughened path, the sunbeam bright
      The hourly thorn and cross.

Thou know all; I lean my head,
      My weary eyelids close;
Content and glad awhile to tread
      This path, since my God knows!

And He has loved me! All my heart
      With answering love is stirred;
And every anguished pain and smart
      Find healing in the word.

So here I lay me down to rest,
      As nightly shadows fall,
And lean, confiding, on His breast,
      Who knows and pities all!
                              —Sunshine in the Soul

CHAPTER 3

Northern Castle Town—Sendai

(1) Shokei Girls School (1917–1927 March)

Miss Allen settled in Shokei Girls School in Sendai, a pleasant and spacious city which is one of the largest castle towns in Northern Japan. In the early eighteenth century, the educational administration of the lord of Sendai had established the institution of higher education for young people.

Shokei Girls School was located in the central area. So the students were very courteous girls from wealthy families. Although Miss Allen was used to a strict way of life from her childhood and at Salah Curtis Home, she was astonished at the atmosphere of the school. The principal, Miss Buzzell (1866–1935), worked in the school from early in the morning to late in the evening. She always quoted the verse from the Bible; "My Father is working still, and I am working." (John 5:17)

30　　BUILD UP, BUILD UP, PREPARE THE ROAD!

* She was a very, very Spartan individual, always wearing long skirts and men's Congress boots, and her hair was pulled back very tightly. Her training was equally severe, and it was hard for the students; and it was just as hard for the other missionaries, especially for me, the only young person out from America. Miss Buzzell was a real pioneer who had known some mighty hard days in her home in Nebraska, days in which grasshoppers had eaten up the entire crop.

Her clothes were so old-fashioned, and here I came fresh out of college with georgette blouses, shorter skirts, and, worst of all, silk stockings. The girls got a great kick out of me, not only because I was so different in age but also different in dress. Once Miss Buzzell said me, "Can't you settle down and put on cotton hose? You'll freeze to death" Well, I soon found out that I was freezing to death, and I put my pride out a little bit! (A. Hem., p. 31–32)

However Miss Allen respected the firm faith and vitality of Miss Buzzell. Miss Buzzell worked very hard to run the school and also to hold many meetings. She had lot of influence on the social and intellectual life in the town. For example, through her English Bible classes, many high school boys became leading figures in the Japanese university education and intellectual world; Sakuzo Yoshino, professor of Tokyo University, Sakusaburo Uchigasaki, professor of Waseda University, and Motoi Kurihara as the president of Kyoto University etc.

Miss Buzzell severed her connection with school after its 25th anniversary, moved to the northern small town of Tono in 1920, and opened up special facilities for women and children of the community and Tono Kindergarten. After her resignation, Shokei still had many difficult problems. Miss Allen stayed for more than ten years, not only to teach at school, but to visit the small country towns near Sendai.

(2) Shinei Kindergarten at Taira (1921–27), Seiko Kindergarten at Shiogama (1922–38)

As a missionary Miss Allen visited small churches in the nearby town, which had been established at the end of nineteenth century, where a few Christians kept their faith in poor conditions. She worked hard to help them and to establish kindergartens in these areas; Seiko Kindergarten in the north of Miyagi Prefecture and Shinei Kindergarten on the seaside of Fukushima Prefecture. Many children attended the kindergartens and they brought back the western life style to their homes; hygiene, preventive medicine, nutrition etc. Country people had been interested in and listened to the talks humbly about the new way of life, but about Christianity, they took an indifferent attitude. As the director of two kindergartens, she traveled to many rural villages in the northern country.

Gradually she began wondering if it would be good as a missionary to live in the city and to teach at a well-equipped school.

At that time she met Toyohiko Kagawa and Inazo Nitobe.

(3) Encounter with Iwate Prefecture;
Dr. I. Nitobe and Dr. T. Kagawa

In the opening address at the Allen Junior College in 1970, Miss Allen said;

> "It was in 1918 when I met for the first time Dr. Nitobe, an administrative vice-minister of the League of Nations. At a dinner party held in Sendai, I learnt that Iwate Prefecture was his native place. He was born as a Samurai's son in Morioka. Through him, I was able to open my eyes to the northern area far from Sendai."

In those days, a cold summer followed every year interminably. Farmers and fishermen could not make enough to live in the small rural villages. In order to pay taxes, they had to leave their home in search of temporary work or sell their own children. She could not close her mind to the scenes of the miserable circumstances without suggesting to them a better way of life. She was so strongly provoked with sympathy for Dr. Nitobe and Dr. Kagawa, and was eager to work as a rural missionary in the country side. She had studied many things from fifteen years of practical experience in Japan. She decided to resign from Shokei Girls' School and take a break for study at Chicago University.

* I finally decided that it was better for me to leave Sendai.

Many missionaries were willing to go there and teach English and do routine work as their calling, but I had become acquainted with country work and it interested me very much. As someone said, I was well-qualified for country work because I had no sense of small, a gift of gab, and I liked Japanese food. Those were my three qualifications! Anyway, I did have those qualities; I liked the country work, I liked the country people, and I liked the country food.

Every experience brings something of real value to us, and one of the greatest things I got out of Sendai was Kuni Obara.... "I am a missionary, but there will always be many things that I cannot do, things that the Japanese will have to do, and I would like to be able to count on you, Kuni. I think you are the one to carry on." (A. Hem., pp. 34-5)

On the journey to America she visited the Bible lands with Kuni Obara, who was an able student and wanted to enroll in Franklin College.

Mr. William Wynd wrote in his book "*Seventy Years in Japan*":

* Miss Thomasine Allen did not stay long in Shokei Girls School, but long enough to make a valuable contribution to its high standing as an educational institution and a center of Christian influence. And she continued her influence after she left the school, for she stayed on in the Tohoku. She was set apart for special work for women who necessitated a great deal of travel. She had thus a unique opportunity of keeping in touch with the graduates of school and of securing their

cooperation in ministering to the needs of those around them. Sometimes the needs of the Tohoku villages were appalling. Foods devastated whole districts, famine followed, and the inarticulate villagers would have died if starvation and pestilence of God had not stirred up the hearts of outsiders to visit them and help them.

In this work Miss Allen has taken a leading part. Her facile pen has enabled the writer to tell of the work of others in Tohoku, but what Lord has done through her in the famine stricken village is not material for history. It comes to light only when the Christian's works "do follow" the worker. (*Seventy Years in Japan*, pp. 227–8 (Mr. William WYND, Privately Printed in N.Y.))

[The Protestant Church in Japan]

After the Meiji Restoration in 1868, the new Japanese government promoted foreign trade and lifted the ban on propagation of Christianity. As a consequence, a lot of foreigners, as members of trading companies or missionaries, entered Japan so that the society was enthusiastic about absorbing the culture of western countries. On the other hand, there were a great number of "Samurai" disbanded from the feudal Lords, so they moved to the new capital of Tokyo from their rural countryside, looking for jobs. Many of them had knocked on the doors of Christian churches. "Samurai" were well versed in both literary and military arts. In the early stages, Christian missionaries could not establish churches, but just private institutions, to where many excellent but employed young people gathered seeking financial dependence. As a result they were able to learn a lot about

I. "Sunshine in the Soul" | 35

western technology as well as Christianity.

During the 1920's there were two streams among the Japanese Protestant Churches. One was characteristic of the urban area and the other of the countryside. Especially in Tokyo, the church was strongly influenced by the theology of Pastor Masahisa Uemura, who was a conservative person. His theology was involved only with the church, the gospel and faith, but was not concerned with social services or moral activities. For this reason, this theology stayed within the members and their children.

On the other hand, the nation had strongly and rapidly changed to an industrial society. Naturally enough, there occurred serious problems of the newly-industrialized nation in various ways. Japanese non-Christian dignitaries were active in agencies of moral and social reform, and they welcomed Christian efforts to solve the problems.

The first person of the Japanese social gospel was Dr. Toyohiko Kagawa. He was baptized when he was sixteen in the countryside of Tokushima. After having a serious illness he moved to the industrial slum in Kobe. His book "*Crossing the Death Line*" brought to light the miserable social conditions and sent shock waves through Japanese Christians. His social gospel was able to be active, not in industrial slums, but in rural life. He and his sympathizers were active in peace movements and in temperance and anti-prostitution organizations. They advocated fair labor laws and did social work among the laboring class. "What can we do for the farmers and fishermen? How can we talk about spiritual life to them?" In the late 1920's he started "The Kingdom of God Movement", supported by the International Missionary Council and the Japanese churches. Its intention was to evangelize farmers and industrial workers. All through his life Dr. Kagawa put many different projects into practice for the poor and the needy.

(4) The University of Chicago

* Many people in America said to me, "If you are going
into country work, why in the world do you want an M.A?
You don't need a master degree for work up there." Well,
you don't, in a way. But I felt that the country needed just
as much as the city; no chain is stronger than its weakest
link. The northern rural areas were very backward, and if we
could raise their level, then the whole chain of Japan would
be stronger. (A. Hem., p. 38)

In 1927 coming back to America, Miss Allen immediately
enrolled in the graduate school of the University of Chicago
to study some work in comparative religions. Although Miss
Allen was able to understand the many kind of religious
functions held in daily life in Japan, she could not accept the
Japanese religion entirely. Shinto, Buddhism, and Confucianism
blended into daily life. Pantheism and Shintoism were the
first religions of Japan, and in the sixth century Buddhism
was introduced along with Confucianism. She comprehended
that Japanese faith introduced was not only based on religious
theory, but folklore or myth of more than two thousand years.
In rural Japan the traditional rites themselves were important
for agriculture and fishery. They believed that harmony with
nature would bring them harvest. Superstitions, lucky days,
lucky directions, and shamanism were important aspects for
all the villagers, whether they believed them or not. "What

I. "Sunshine in the Soul" | 37

do Japanese believe?" Nobody could answer correctly, so Miss Allen wanted to find out the answer. She had heard, "The northern part has no history, only legends." There were keys to understand the Japanese religion.

> * The courses on comparative religions were especially helpful to me because they offered me the opportunity to delve deeper into the religions of Japan and into the religions of other countries related to Japan. Under Dr. Hayden I wrote my thesis, "Religious Educational Values of Japanese Folklore. It demanded a great deal of reading and research, and that was all very beneficial and helpful to me in my work in the years to come. (A. Hem., p. 39)

In the University of Chicago, at the same time, Miss Allen learned pragmatic theory of education from Dr. John Dewey (1859–1952), who had established a laboratory school aiming toward the realization of his theory. Afterward, based on it, Miss Allen established several schools in Kuji.

I want to add that she was greatly influenced by Sir. Rabindranath Tagore, who was awarded the Nobel prize for Literature in 1913. He visited Japan the following year when she came to Japan.

II

"To Sow the Seeds, To Try to Follow up on Results"

[Poem 2]

DWELL DEEP

Thomasine Allen

Dwell deep,
    my soul, dwell deep!
I am not my body,
    my body is only the physical
    house in which I live.
The essential thing about me
    is my spiritual life.
So long as I am honest
    and true and trust in God,
    my soul is beyond
    the reach of all adversity.
No, no trouble can touch
    the essential and eternal "me".
Because I am God's child
    I can meet all that comes
    in the day's work
    bravely and serenely.

CHAPTER I

"Go where the need is greatest": Morioka (1929–38)

(1) Uchimaru Kindergarten: Protect Children and Women

Miss Allen went back to Japan immediately after she received her master's degree in 1929. During the voyage she felt like going back to her own home country, she wrote. As soon as she arrived in Japan, she succeeded Miss Buzzell as director of Tono Kindergarten in Iwate Prefecture. After a while, she moved to Uchimaru kindergarten in Morioka, the capital of Iwate. In Morioka, she had to live in an old Japanese house, cooking and keeping warm with charcoal fire pots. The Japanese houses were built mostly of straw, wood and paper. How could they live when it was fifteen degrees below zero outside? It was the life style of the Japanese at that time. Once settled in at Morioka Miss Allen found herself busy with three different types of work.

At first, Miss Allen had to supervise the Uchimaru

Kindergarten, and worked closely with the mothers' club. Secondly, in 1929, the women in Morioka protested against the Morioka prefectural assembly, which decided to try to move every house of prostitution to the center of the city. Against this resolution, Miss Allen and the mothers of the kindergarten and Christian women worked together to collect signatures on the streets in the cold wind. She said that she was surprised that most of the men were indifferent to this problem. Also she thought that a better moral education was necessary to build a happy home. Afterwards, a famous Japanese poet Kotaro Takamura dedicated a sympathetic poem for this women's movement. Thirdly, she opened a Christian Center at Morioka Shinjo.

(2) Morioka Shinjo Christian Center (1930–38)

Twelve months later, in 1930, Kuni Obara finished her university education in the States, and came back to Morioka. When she was in Tokyo, some Christian school offered her a high position. But she refused it. "I felt that I wanted to spend my life where it would count for more, and where other people were not willing to go. So I joined forces with Miss Allen and went to Morioka." (K. Hem., p. 47)"

With Kuni Obara's help, Miss Allen founded the Shinjo Christian Center at the edge of town. The two women started various activities in the center for boys and girls, equally for mothers and young people. We can count up to more than

II. *"To Sow the Seeds, To Try to Follow up on Results"* | 43

seven clubs shown in records and pictures. Some young girls from the country side came to live at the Center and learned how to help Miss Allen and how to teach children. Finally, Homare Kindergarten was opened.

(3) Community Evangelism (1929–37)

She was released from teaching responsibilities, so she was free to work in the Baptist churches near Morioka. There were several small churches in Hanamaki, Kamaishi, Taira, Kesennuma, and Hachinohe. Often her reports told honestly about these churches:

> "The church here is probably less adequately equipped to meet its opportunity than any in northern Japan." Sometimes the reports were encouraging: "From an organization that had to be practically carried, they have grown into a group that makes and carries out its own plans." (A. Hem., p. 48)

However, her latest plan was to establish a neighborhood center and a day nursery in a rural area where there was no church. What provoked Miss Allen into the community evangelism of small villages to the northern area, in spite of her working very busily in Morioka? She could not ignore the miserable lives of the peasants and fishermen in the isolated small villages. From 1929 to 1937, during every summer vacation, she held summer schools at Morioka, Numakunai, Hanamaki, Matsuokozan, Takadamatsubara, and Kuji. These projects were established by her own ideas, so it was noted as a different activity from the fundamental missionary plan.

> * It's not exactly fair to call it a Daily Vacation Bible school, I guess, when they didn't know anything about the Bible. With six or seven workers I stayed in each village for a week or ten days, usually living in the public school. Each day four or five hundred children came to the school. (A. Hem., p. 48)

In every year, this program gradually became a regular delightful event in the village, so not only children and mothers, but civil servants were waiting for it. On May 1931, a permanent day nursery was opened.

> * Doors of all kinds were open to us, so that it was not just a vacation school for children, but it reached out and touched all of the community. Two afternoons a week I conducted cooking classes for the women. That sounds big, and those who know my limitations will doubtless be overcome with mirth or surprise, or both! Some of the women had asked beforehand if I would teach them some foreign cooking, and I became proficient in fixing rice cakes, omelets, and Spanish rice, teaching about eight or nine dishes in all. Even though I may be accused of boasting, I will say that it was a huge success.
>
> Every night we had meetings for the young men, conducted by Mr. Imai, the Morioka pastor preceded by an hour of hymn practice. They never seemed to tire of singing! The young women asked if they, too, might have a chance to learn

some hymns, so two night were given to them for hymns and a talk. When I asked if they would like to play some games, they clapped their hands in glee just like children, for there was so little joy or color in their life. (A. Hem., p. 48)

= Summer School and Summer Chrismas in Matsuo Kozan=

Matsuo Kozan was a mining town filled with a horrible scent of sulfur, where three thousand people lived, and the men worked in the mines. When going up to the town from Morioka, after getting off a train at the small station, people had to climb a steep path on foot for two hours. The town was built for the mines, where there were neither trees nor flowers. The sulfur fumes ruined the plants and trees.

[Report 2] =memo undated
Christmas in July

Thomasine Allen

It was during the year 1931 that Christmas came in July. The theme for the children's school was Love, and the motto was John 3: 16. Each day there were stories of the love of God. There were five classes with an average of sixty children to each class, and each class prepared one of scenes of the Christmas pageant. Excitement mounted as the children made a gold paper crown for Herod and turned Japanese carrying cloths into Palestinian headdresses. When the big night came, all the citizens of Matsuo Kozan were on hand for their first Christmas pageant.

After the pageant came the party. Producing Christmas

decorations for the party in July on the top of a sulfur mountain in Japan was a challenge. An old Christmas card from America provided pictures of camels and wise men which were mimeographed on sheets of paper and then made up into bags for candy. The mountain children knew few of the sweets that children in the cities enjoyed, and the found the Christmas bags of candy a rare treat. At the end of the evening, the adults stayed to clean the stage, to pack away the costumes, and to clean and scrub the floors.

When we left at the week's end, children accompanied us down to the road.

= Summer School at Sanriku Rias Coast in Iwate Prefecture =
In 11th March 2011, the huge Tsunami destroyed all over these shoreline. Only one pine tree of the seventy thousand others stood bravely and beautifully on the sea shore.

Iwate Prefecture is the largest mountainous area and has the coldest winter in the main island of Japan. The coastline was a beautiful rias coast, but was separated by steep mountains from the center of the Prefecture. The road wasn't paved, and there was only a narrow pass covered with slippery mud to cross over the peak to the shoreline. There were no bridges or tunnels. The very sharp cross road was called "Sen-nin Mountain". It meant where "a benevolent wizard lived." The automobile was not in common use, so Miss Allen had to walk up and down on foot with the villagers. She put "waraji" (the old Japanese style straw sandal) on her own shoes, so as not to slide and fall

II. "To Sow the Seeds, To Try to Follow up on Results" | 47

down. She recollected a pleasant feeling seeing the panorama from the top of the hill and having delicious Japanese lunches with her comrades. She visited and had the summer schools on several sea shores every year. Afterward in a report, she wrote about the summer school in the forest of seventy thousand pine trees, and more than two hundred children gathered there.

While Miss Allen worked from village to village with all her strength, war broke out in China. Japan's relations with America were going from bad to worse day by day, and the Japanese people kept away from foreigners. All the same, she never stopped talking about God's Love no matter what happened.

It was 1933, when Mr. Takeshi Yahaba met Miss Allen on the street in Morioka. Amazed by her works, he decided to study again at a theological seminary, and was baptized. He had a strong will to help her work. Several years later, he joined Miss Allen in Kuji and devoted his life to supporting her work. He married Kuni Obara during the wartime.

CHAPTER 2

Damage from Cold Weather and the Great Tsunami (1931–34)

(1) Poor Harvest and Starvation

In 1931 starvation was prevalent all over the northland. Spring came late, and the sun didn't thaw the frozen fields, so peasants could not plow and seed the paddies. Temperatures were low throughout spring. Also in summer, a dense fog had covered the muddy fields and tiny plants. Before harvest time, the cold winter had come again. It was a time of hunger and starvation for the villagers.

In addition, financial difficulties of the nation had adverse effects on living conditions even in the countryside. The local finance, which was dependent on the transportation of rice and silk thread, was damaged hard by the American financial panic in 1929. It was the worst famine. Cities overflowed with unemployed people, and the countryside, with death by starvation. The rightist movements were becoming stronger,

II. "To Sow the Seeds, To Try to Follow up on Results" | 49

and in 1931, the Japanese government sent the Japanese army to attack China. The relationship with America was going to deteriorate, so that most Japanese people looked at foreigners with suspicion and hostility. However Miss Allen set on a trip to make a survey of the famine in the countryside with a few comrades.

> * I took trip, walking all over Iwate Ken, but especially the very poor area along the seashore. There was no other way to get there, and we walked fifty mile over nothing but mountain paths where there were no roads. I'm positive that there was not one bit of level ground in the whole fifty miles—not an inch! I had never seen mountain until I was grown, because I lived in Indiana where it was very flat, and for me to walk fifty miles over a highland path was really something. We came to one peak, the top of which seemed to reach to the heavens. We were told that it was called Mount Resignation because the prefectural officials had gotten that far and said, "We would rather resign than climb that mountain," I knew what they meant, and I understood their feelings—but we climbed that mountain, and many more. (A. Hem., pp. 60–61)

After coming back to Morioka, she wrote to American and Japanese friends how miserable the living conditions of the northern famine were. She then asked for their help in contributing something toward these people. Her letter was published in the "Japan Advertiser," and soon large quantities of relief goods and lots of money poured in from various places.

* I was quite astonished, for I had no idea of doing all that! The next thing was to administer the supplies, and that was a big job. We tried to distribute the things as justly as possible. Sometimes it was better to give money and sometimes it was better to send food or clothes. All this took a great deal of time, but it gave us wonderful contacts with the people. (A. Hem., pp. 60–61)

Miss Allen and her staff visited from door to door delivering the relief goods to the isolated small villages on foot, carrying big luggage on their backs, and carrying two pieces of luggage in their hands.

* The people we met would say, "What are you selling?" I would reply, "Oh, heaven I'm selling nothing! I'm trying to give this away; it's heavy!" …

In Tayama the school principal was the contact man. He told the relief team that Tayama had never had to ask for help before, but this year sixty one of his pupils were in desperate need of food, and two hundred were in need of clothing. These little children came to school after a breakfast of broth with a little barley and a few finely cut radish leaves. They had no lunch, and they went home to a supper of same broth. "Yet they come to school regularly," said the principal, "and it is all I can do to keep back the tears as I stand before them." Before the food and clothing distribution he spoke to his ragged and hungry charges: "We have never had to receive help before, but this year has been unusual in the failure of rice crop. Up to now we have not

II. "To Sow the Seeds, To Try to Follow up on Results" | 51

received anything, and these ladies representing Christianity are the very first to relieve our need. You must not think that you can receive things or depend upon others all the time. This winter could not help it, but, as soon as spring comes, you must work hard in order to help yourself and others. And every morning you should thank God for his kindness to you.

When we stood looking down into their little pitiful, sallow, earnest and attentive faces, and knowing that they were oh, so hungry, the tears streamed down our cheeks. Then the principal lined them up, called out their names, and told us what to give, for he had looked up the needs of each home. The children came to us solemnly in their ragged kimonos, and with many bows received their little bundles of food and clothes. As I stood giving out the food, my feet, encased in several layers of wool, were so cold I could scarcely stand it. Although it was ten degrees below zero, I saw several barefoot children and others in ragged socks, and then I was heartily ashamed of myself for even thinking about my own feet. (A. Hem., pp. 61–62)

The mayor of a district with three small villages wrote a letter to her asking for her help. This district was five miles from the nearest train station, and was covered with snow.

* First we stopped to see an old man nearly blind with trachoma. He could see just enough to weave crude straw leggings which brought him an income of about five sen (penny) a day. On this he supported his little six-year-old orphaned granddaughter and himself. Their food was mostly

barley and water, and he had no fire. Friends had brought him a little brushwood from the mountains, but he was saving that to cook his food and could not afford to have a fire to keep them warm. His clothes were ragged, and he was barefooted, and of course there were no mats on the floor. He would put his hands against his body to warm them when they got too cold to work; and, if the cold was too terrible, he would climb into some straw. We left clothing for him and for the little girl, and later we made arrangements to supply them with fuel.

In another place we visited, we found four orphaned children living alone, the oldest of whom was a boy of fifteen. A short time before our visit the youngest, a child of four, was taken suddenly ill and died in the night. Without telling anyone, the other children got a box, put the body inside, and said a prayer to Jizo-San; and the boy put the box on his back, took a spade, and together they quietly buried their little sister.

But relief work was not all snow, wind, and cold. There was sunshine, too, for the fortitude and bravery of the unfortunate and the privilege of taking them a bit of warmth and cheer was most rewarding. However, they, too, found ways their contribution.

One night we found ourselves in a tiny village too tired to walk another step, and we sought shelter in a farmer's hut. "Why," he said, "we do not even have lights, and our home is too poor. Please go on to the next village." We told him that we had candles with us, and we asked him please just give us shelter. He guided us to his house and broke the news to his wife labored with him in the open all day. She hastened to put down some mats on the floor and to fix a fire. Pine twigs burning in a kettle furnished the heat and about as much smoke as warmth. We lit our candles, one by one, and felt that we were in another generation as sat around the little fire and talked with our host and his family. Never had we been treated with greater hospitality and courtesy. They gave their best and we appreciated it to the utmost.

The glow of that fire remains in my heart to this day. At the end of that long mountain trip was Kuji. We had gone along the coast, through all of the coastal villages, and Kuji was the end. That summer we decided that we would have one of our vacation village Bible school in Kuji, so my first contact here goes back to 1931. (A. Hem., pp. 62–63)

(2) The Great Sanriku Tsunami (1933)

On March 3, 1933, a terrible tsunami attacked the beautiful northern sea shore in Tohoku. A lot of small villages were completely destroyed by the great earthquake and were washed away by the big tidal wave. Those were the places where Miss Allen had held the summer schools, and her group for famine relief had walked and visited.

* Two years after that, in 1933, there was a terrible tidal wave that completely washed out several villages. Many lives were lost and much damage was done, so we started out on another relief tri, and we walked through many of the same places. One little village where we had slept one night with "the most hearty welcome" during our first trip was completely wiped out, and there was nothing left but the school

54　　BUILD UP, BUILD UP, PREPARE THE ROAD!

building; everything else was gone. We administered food as
we walked on and on, helping the people and making wonderful contacts with the authorities in Iwate Prefecture. At
the end of that trip, too Kuji. (A. Hem., p. 63)

Coming back to Morioka, Miss Allen could not forget the
horrible scene of the villages suffering from heavy damage
from the tsunami. Most of all, she was very concerned about
the children who were hungry and cold, and the children who
lived poorly clothed. If they didn't know "how to be loved",
they would never understand "how to love" and never could
have the hope to enjoy their lives. She began to think about
leaving Morioka for a small country town where no Christian
missionary work had existed. That was Kuji.

　* Sometimes the needs of the Tohoku villages were appall-
　ing. Floods devastated whole districts, famine followed, and
　the inarticulate villagers would have died if starvation and
　pestilence of God had not stirred up the hearts of outsiders
　to visit them and help them. In this work Miss Allen has
　taken a leading part. Her facile pen has enabled the writer
　to tell of the work of others in the Tohoku but what the
　Lord has done through her in the famine stricken villages
　is not material for history. It comes to light only when the
　Christian's works "do follow" the worker. ("*Seventy Years in
　Japan*" W. Wynd, 1941, N.Y., p. 228)

CHAPTER 3

❧

The Layman's Missionary Inquiry (1932–38)

* It was this program that caught the attention of the Re-Thinking Mission group. They were so intent upon Christianity not being just an ivory tower and not being confined within the wall of the church. They thought that Christians should get out among those who know nothing at all, to sow the seed and to try to follow up results. (A. Hem., p. 50)

The Layman's Missionary Inquiry was formed as an interdenominational organization in 1931. It had the intention to survey and to evaluate the results of one hundred years of American Protestant Mission in Asia, which was started in the nineteenth century by the large donations from many laymen. But early in the twentieth century, the international circumstances had changed rapidly. The state of affairs was greatly confused under colonialism, industrialism, capitalism and communism etc. In spite of disorder, the Inquiry was

56 | BUILD UP, BUILD UP, PREPARE THE ROAD!

organized under the chairmanship of Dr. William E. Hocking, Professor of Philosophy at Harvard University with a committee of fifteen laymen. In 1932 they published the results of their work in a book, "*Re-Thinking Missions*". In 1932 the committee members came to Japan, and researched the Japanese churches, and concluded as follows:

> They deplored that the lack of rural participation in the church in Japan and urgently recommended that agricultural mission be organized No mission board, noted the laymen, had ever sent an agricultural missionary to Japan. Missionary evangelists had been assigned to country work and succeeded in establishing churches in a few small towns and villages. There was little money for the country, for mission funds were usually committed to maintaining urban work, and there was little to spare for rural evangelism. (Hem., p. 52)

[Document 1]

DR. CHARLES P EMERSON

INDIANAPOLIS

October 18, 1932,

Miss Thomasine Allen,
Morioka, Japan.

My dear Miss Allen:

It was delightful to get your letter and records of your summer course.

Please don't think that I am flattering you but I do want to tell you that in our commission you stood out as

II. "To Sow the Seeds, To Try to Follow up on Results" | 57

one of the three or four missionaries of the Orient whose work thoroughly appealed to us. That certainly is a record of which to be proud. The members of the commission often spoke of you at their various meetings since we left Japan.

We stopped off two weeks at Honolulu in order to get our thoughts on paper and the last two weeks of August met on the Maine Coast at Rockland for further work on the report, which was finished at Lake MO honk during the middle of September, and has been presented to the directors who sent us. Of course time only can tell what the results of the commissioner's work will be, but we are rather proud that the report was unanimous and was made unanimous without the necessity of omitting any recommendations on which we could not agree. We had a wonderful trip. We only hope that the missionaries might benefit by our work as much as we profited by and enjoyed our visit to them, but that would be asking a great deal, for we thoroughly enjoyed every minute.

I was so interested in what I heard about your work. The one wish I had was that I might also be on the foreign field but that dates back to my college days. I would much rather have been one of those visited than a visitor.

Mrs. Emerson was greatly pleased with the piece of silk you sent her. She enjoyed the trip, although was obliged to omit the last month because two of our children were graduating from school and one of us had to be present. Our oldest daughter has finished college, Charles Jr., is in his Senior year at Princeton University, Perry is in his Freshman year at Cornell, while the two youngest girls are at Tudor Hall at Indianapolis.

Indiana is in the midst of the depression and also of one of the most vigorous political fights of which I have any

58 BUILD UP, BUILD UP, PREPARE THE ROAD!

recollection.

Wishing you the best of success as well as great happiness in your work, I am,

Sincerely yours,

Charles P. Emerson

CPE/c

[Report 3]

In Pine Grove and Temple Grounds

The lines of the poem:
This is the forest primeval

The murmuring pine came to mind when walking thru the wide stretch of fantastically shaped pine trees—a grove about two miles in length on the edge of the sandy ocean, beach. This fringe of pines is a half hour walk from the town of Takada which nestles between the mountains and the sea. Words fail in attempting to describe one of the most picturesque spots in all picturesque Japan. It is called Matsubara or Pine Field and is classified as one of the 100 most beautiful places in Japan. If this 'Pine Field' were in the southern part of Japan it would soon become a tourist spot, but situated as it is way off the beaten track, and until a few months ago with not even train connection, it is not known, and so is still 'primeval'. In this lovely place, to the music of the 'murmuring pines' accompanied by the beat of the ocean waves, we had a summer school for nearly 500 Takasa children—who with a possible few exceptions heard from us for the first time about Jesus and His Kingdom of Love.

And how did we happen to go there? One day a former

II. "To Sow the Seeds, To Try to Follow up on Results" | 59

member of the Iwate Legislature called—a representative from the district in which Takasa is located. He suggested our having a summer Bible School in the Takasa pine grove for as he said, "There is no Christian work being done in that whole district." Many, many years ago missionaries and Japanese pastors toured this country, walking from place to place and holding meetings, but for various reasons the work could not be followed up and a generation has now arisen 'who knew not Joseph. The Legislature member offered to meet me at Takasa and introduce me to the 'powers that be". So in June I made the preliminary trip, being the first foreign woman most of the town had ever seen. The mayor and his staff seemed most anxious for us to come and offered to let us live in the matted sewing rooms of the Government Girls' High School, to save expense.

When the day in August finally came for us to start I must confess that I felt a real sympathy with Jonah in wanting to flee—for the responsibility of our little band of eight trying to represent Jesus in a town that knew him not seemed too great to bear. Of course we did not know how many children would come for many country people still have a real prejudice against the name of Christianity. But if there were any prejudice we certainly did not encounter it for we were shown the greatest courtesy the whole time, even the Nichiren Buddhist priest showered us daily with kindnesses (his home and temple in the pine grove.) Upon our arrival, after having been met and escorted to the H.S. building which with mattresses and mosquito nets lent by citizens, was to be our home for a week, two of us went out to make the official calls on the mayor, the city office, the principals of the schools, and the police headquarters. Then that evening the Mayor and one of the principals called on us. After these formalities were over we were ready to start to work—and it was work indeed, for about 500 children came from kindergarten to H. S. age. We had the flag raising and worship service (first having to teach some songs for it was their first experience) all together, the children sitting on the sand under the pine trees. Then we divided into eight classes, with one teacher carrying for about 60 or more children—each class marching with their teacher to its own group of trees which formed lovely 'class rooms'. There was plenty of room, the ceiling reached to the blue sky, and no walls kept out the salt breeze from the ocean. Our theme was, Citizens of the Kingdom of Love, and this we worked out in a group of seven lessons. There were no specialists in handcraft and no equipment so each teacher had to care for her or his own flock during that period making the most of her bit of knowledge or as in my case, lack of knowledge. One of the men teachers dyed sand and had his class make sand pictures. Another had each of her 85 children bring a bit of cheap white material and taught hemstitching—how to make hemstitched sleeves for the under kimono, covers for the table in the home etc. Another made toys out of old materials the children could bring—and other classes made the backgrounds and properties for the religious drama to be given on the last night. Then there was a play period for each class and gymnastic exercises to music for the whole large group, and a half hour of teaching songs. Then came the dinner, when we formed in a huge double circle and ate our rice balls together. This was followed by a brief rest period, lying under the trees, and then came the bathing and swimming in the ocean, under the expert direction of our

II. "To Sow the Seeds, To Try to Follow up on Results" | 61

three men teachers. Living so near the ocean we thought this would not be any treat for the children but it was the first time for many to go in this year, so great was the hilarity and fun on the part of the children, worry on the part of the women teachers, and constant vigilance on the part of the young men. In addition to this daily program we had a meeting for mothers and two meetings for the young women of the town. And on the last night we invited the town's people to the children's program held in the primary school, the chief part of which was the drama of David and Saul in four acts. In accordance with our general theme, Citizens of the Kingdom of Love, forgiving ones' enemies was one of the subjects and this was portrayed in David forgiving Saul.

The next morning after doing up all our baggage and making all the 'thank-you' calls on officials and others, we looked forward to having two or three hours on the beach, free of responsibility, but an invitation came from the mayor for us to attend a dinner to be given in our honor. This with the waiting, with the speeches etc. consumed three hours so our free time had to be sacrificed on the altar of politeness. The little station was filled to overflowing with people to see us off, many bringing gifts and all urging us to return next year. The children were lined up and sang in farewell one of the songs we had taught them. As our train pulled out, starting on our seven hour trip back to Morioka, the mayor, his staff, school teachers, mothers and children all waved goodbye, the latter running along with the train crying, "Sayonara, Please come again next year".

The school in the Morioka Temple Grounds was held the week preceding the Takasa Pine Grove one. It was the third year for this school and the attendance has increased each year, this year 170 handing in enrollment blanks. Under the direction of Miss Obara the daily program with the children from 7:00 to 4:30 (but for the teachers 6:30 to late at night) was efficiently carried out. This was the first year to have H. S. boys' class and they proved most helpful in carrying drinking water and doing the heavier tasks. On the last day many mothers came to see the exhibition of handwork and the David and Saul drama. Here the grassy stage under the tall cryptomeria was large enough for the kindergarten 'sheep' to be herded by the two human dogs and rescued from the prowling 'lion' by David's sling. The scene of David, playing the harp before King Saul was a bit marred by the scratching of mosquito bites upon the part of the little bare legged courtiers—for while natural stages are indeed beautiful, they do have certain drawbacks.

May I close with the words of one of the Takata mothers, who came every day to our school: "Some country people have a prejudice against the name of Christianity, but from all you have taught us I think it is a most beautiful and challenging religion. Please teach us more."

Thomasine Allen

CHAPTER 4

My Home Town—Kuji

Kuji was located in the most isolated area of Iwate Prefecture, where there was no Christian missionary work, neither schools, nor social settlements, nor agriculture missions.

Miss Allen made the decision to open a kindergarten there. It was obvious that she would encounter a lot of obstacles and financial difficulties. However, Miss Allen decided to live in Kuji. She felt that the mutual confidence she had established with the local government people through the relief activities in this area should help. She felt that it might be the last chance for her to promote her works there. The mothers in Kuji had been very appreciative of her work at the day nursery and the summer school. They asked her enthusiastically if she would be able to establish a kindergarten. The town agreed with them and the mayor said that his people needed leadership training.

(1) The Trip to the United States

Miss Allen made application to the Japan Baptist Mission extended program. The financial problem was crucial, but she was at least able to secure her salary and a working budget. Of course she did not expect more money for her new mission work, only their blessing. During the American economic depression, the ABFMS and WABFMS were facing their worst financial crisis. Donations in 1935 were half of what they had been in 1931. "The Board came to realize that genuine disaster threatened the entire work unless resources were promptly increased, or unless the work as a whole was readjusted to a narrower base.

> * Dr. William Axling, member of the JBM expressed the anguish of missionaries in the field; "This is tragic for those of us out here on the firing line." (Hem. p. 65)

Miss Allen took two weeks' vacation going back to the States. It was surely a trip devoted to appealing for contributions. While staying in America, she visited as many churches and groups as possible, to tell what she had done so far, and what she would like to do in the future. Her stories made deep impressions on listeners, and a lot of money and relief goods were sent to Kuji. Although she felt anti-Japanese feelings were mounting throughout the United States, she departed to

II. "To Sow the Seeds, To Try to Follow up on Results" | 65

Japan leaving her aged mother at home. After coming back to Morioka, she sent letters of appreciation to her friends, which were published in the journal "Baptist Observer". Generous responses were expanded.

[Report 4]

The Baptist Observer

December 2, 1937

Dear Friends in the Homeland:

There is something majestic and withal a bit lonely about a big ship slipping out silently at midnight. No big crowds, paper streamers, sounding gong nor playing band, but instead, the lights of the sleeping city sending out their colored reflections in the rippling water, the men on the little tug boat which had come to turn us around, shouting out into the dark stillness, "O. K. Captain?" and the response, "Hai, Hai, O. K." and then we were definitely putting out to sea.

My goodbyes to the many Los Angeles friends had been said in the afternoon and evening when they came the long distance to the boat, so at midnight as I stood on the deck of the slowly outgoing steamer I not only thanked them again, silently, for the loving hospitality extended to me during the two weeks, but remembered with a thankful heart the many, many friends who had made my sojourn in America the past year such a happy, glorious one. And so as always, in the comings and goings to and fro, sadness and gladness are mingled and there is a wish that he could work on both continents, Asia and America.

Due to some cancellations there were only nine

passengers on the big cargo boat and fortunately I had a large stateroom all to myself. This gave me a chance to have some real rest that I sorely needed. In our little group there was a Japanese man who had not been back to his native land for 29 years. He has been a chemist in a laboratory in N.J. and another man and his wife who had not been back for 24 years. What were their feelings as they again saw Mt. Fuji! A young Methodist missionary from Kobe proved the old song, "The Methodists and Baptists are just going along."

The voyage was truly like the Voyage of Life—with some days calm and peaceful, cloudless skies overhead and beautiful blue ocean underneath, then grey skies and choppy seas and a dense fog over all so that we could not see the way we were going, but did know our guide and pilot—and then the friends waiting on the other shore!

Obara San and Yahaba San had taken a 14 hour journey, sitting up all night, in order to meet me. Our boat got in at five o'clock in the evening—and then all 27 pieces of baggage had to be opened (all duty free) and we were ready to drop. The next day we returned to Morioka and there were over fifty people, young and old, down to the station to welcome me back home. The next day Obara San went with me and we made about thirty calls of greeting. The following morning we arose at four and left on a five thirty train for our summer school at the Pine Grove place which so many of you hear me tell about. I missed the Morioka school under the cryptomeria which was held the first week in August, so I was more than glad that I could begin this my fourth period of service with the children under the Pine Trees, and on the shores of the Pacific Ocean. Someway it made you people on the other shore seen a bit nearer.

II. "To Sow the Seeds, To Try to Follow up on Results" | 67

Upon our return to Morioka the freight had arrived and all had to be opened and admired—and presents wrapped, and given. The work has progressed under Obara san's guidance. She has had many problems but has met them with her usual fortitude and ability, and in the spirit of her Master.

Many have been the expressions of joy over the gift for our building. Due to the unsettled conditions, which you all know about, we feel that we must wait till things are more normal before attempting to build. In the meantime we shall be making our definite plans.

May I close this lengthy letter with another Thank You to you all who made my furlough such a happy one, and to all who contributed to make my children here happy.

It is a different country from the one I left just a short year ago, and clouds are thick and dense. When, oh when will the sun break thru the darkness and rise with healing in its wings!

Sincerely
Thomasine Allen
19 Shike, Morioka, Japan

(2) Move to Kuji

In 1938 Miss Allen moved to Kuji, and rented an old Japanese style house at a very low rate, because it was said to be a haunted house. "Did you meet ghosts at night?" Miss Allen laughed and said, "I want to see them. Perhaps they would be astonished to come across me and run away immediately." The awful winter was gone. March was the girl's festival month. She decorated "Ohinasama" (Japanese dolls) on a special stairs of seven steps in her old house. Hinamatsuri is the Japanese doll festival for girls, held on March 3rd.

> * Several of the women said that it was the first time they had ever seen the doll festival, and it was hard to believe! But they had always lives in this backward district, and they had never had such opportunity. People in cities could see the dolls in the shop windows, but country people did not even have this privilege. (A. Hem., p. 68)

Kuji kindergarten was officially opened in April 1938, at the old Japanese style house. The little kindergarten became full with children immediately, and a second kindergarten had to be opened in Okawame, which was about five miles away from Kuji. As the director, Miss Allen visited three times a week.

> * I rode my bicycle out there at least two or three times a week and sometimes every day. Frequently the wind would be so strong against me that I had to pump going downhill. Then I'd think, "Maybe the wind will be at my back coming home, and I can just sail along." But almost invariably the wind would have switched, and I'd have almost as much trouble getting back as I had had going!" (A. Hem., p. 68)

People in this area did not have any chance to see foreigners and to know about the western style life, not to mention Christianity. At first they accepted Miss Allen just from

II. "To Sow the Seeds, To Try to Follow up on Results" | 69

curiosity. Naturally, gradually they came to her to find something new in her way of life. In 1940 a famous writer of children's literature, Temma Nobechi visited Kuji to tell a Bible
story in the kindergarten. Here is a strange picture; Mr.
Nobechi sat on a little chair in the rear car attached and pulled
by bicycle, because he could not walk freely.

Miss Allen thought that she must find land on which to
put the new Kindergarten building. Already, Mr. and Mrs.
Merrell Vories had promised financial and technical support
through his Omi Architecture Department. At first, Miss
Allen had to look for the land.

> * The Kindergarten was housed in a terribly dark dirty
> Japanese house. We had no toys or playthings; only a swing
> made of a piece of rope hung from the limb of tree. We had
> no chairs either, but we were able to pick up some tangerine
> crates, and we brought them to use as stools. We did have
> snakes in the yard, but we finally killed most of them. Worse
> than anything else, however, we had to use this terribly dark,
> unsanitary room for the children.
>
> No one wanted to sell land to Christian, and, after days
> and days of walking and conferring and trying our best to
> find a place, we were about to give up. Then an old woman
> in the country at the edge of Kuji said, "Well, I've heard that
> Christianity is a pretty good religion. I don't know anything
> about it; but they are working for God, and we believe in
> gods, so maybe it's the same. Anyway, I will let them have a
> part of this land." Other people hear about this and talked
> it over, and finally, seven people in all decided to let us have

some ground, and we were able to buy an acre of land at the edge of Kuji. When we were going through all this hardship we couldn't help wondering if it were God' Will for us to stay here. It just seemed as though everything was against us, and yet we had a firm feeling that it was His will, so we went on. What was the best thing to do? What was His will for us in this place? (A. Hem., p. 69)

When the plan for the new building had been drawn by Merrell Vories, Miss Allen was summoned to the police office. The chief of police said to her that the land had to be sold to the Kobe Iron company, who demanded to build a railroad from the iron sand mine to a new factory on the sea side.

> * I told him that I did not see how we could give up the land, so he let me go home and then called in Takeshi. He thought that surely Japanese would not hold out, even though an American might. Takeshi was down there for three hours talking to the chief of police, and bravely he told the man, "We are going to do greater work for Japan than you or the government can possibly do." One didn't talk that way and get away with in 1938, but he did. (A. Hem., p. 70)

(3) Mr. Vories comes to help

The Omi Architecture started the construction of the kindergarten under the supervision of Mr. Vories, who helped Miss Allen not only by donations but by designing the building. Mr. Vories said, "An educational facility must be a healthy and

II. "To Sow the Seeds, To Try to Follow up on Results" | 71

beautiful building, but also awake the spirit of people who live there. It has to guide the people to 'goodness' ".

There were many difficulties in the construction site; the lack of materials was very serious, carpenters came to Kuji but none of them stayed more than a few days because the intricacy of western building was beyond their capacity and the supervision was too strict for them. At last a carpenter in Kuji offered to work on the construction until it would be finished. He said that he would not mind if she would trust him, and he would never blame her for anything. He promised Miss Allen that he would be staying with her to the end.

Actually, in 1940, he completed the kindergarten building and in later years he built thirteen buildings under the Omi Architecture Company. His name was Testuo Hiraya. The moving of the kindergarten finished in June 1941. On September 4th Miss Allen resigned as the director of the kindergarten because Japan-United States relations were worsening.

[Report 5]

We Have Built

Perhaps it may not be inappropriate when ruthless destruction of buildings seems to be the order of the day, to pause a moment and give thanks that one lovely building in a far-away corner of the world has been erected to further the Kingdom of God.

The year—(and it has taken a year to put up the building) of difficulties such as procuring workmen and materials, especially nails; the terrific rise in prices and other seemingly insurmountable obstacles, has been effaced in the joy of fulfillment, and our building which for months seemed to be a Building of Tears has proved to be a real Building of Triumph. How better describe it than in the words of a policeman, "It is like a bit of heaven"; or as a friend so beautifully expressed it, "The building is a miracle. In its simplicity and beauty it reveals the character of Jesus. As I walked thru it I could see Him standing there in the midst of that drab village stretching out His loving arms to bless all who enter its doors."

And many are entering! They come from far and near to see the buildings—old and young—for they have never seen anything so lovely. There is much "oh-in and ah-in" over it all—the large circle room with its many windows giving light and cheer; the classrooms and their welcoming toys and pictures; the sun porch and lovely Japanese room for mothers' meetings; the library upstairs with its windows overlooking mountains, rice-fields, and river—so complete in every way except books! (But anyway we have lots of shelves and are gradually accumulating books); and finally the living quarters for three Japanese teachers.

When the new term opened in April we were perplexed as to what to do. We had only planned for fifty in the kindergarten and after that number was reached, here came mothers with their children asking to enter. It was hard to refuse so we went up to sixty and then made a waiting list. "It is all right if my child does not have a chair, please just let her come anyway" was heard from many. The opening day of kindergarten the building was filled with mothers, fathers,

II. "To Sow the Seeds, To Try to Follow up on Results" | 73

grandparents, and brothers and sisters.

Our acre of ground is at the edge of Kuji so we can minister to the country-side and to a nearby village as well as Kuji. On Sunday morning not only the kindergarten children but about two hundred of all ages, come from all directions along the roads and across the fields to Sunday school. "Seeing all the children come I wanted to come, too", said a teacher in the public school who lives near, and she has been a faithful attendant. Rain does not deter them but increases our problems as it is "some job" to tend to all those shoes (for all shoes must be removed before entering), umbrellas and dirty feet!

Our purpose we had putting up a really attractive building was to show the people here a better way to live materially as well as spiritually—to try to bring a bit of beauty into all this drab ugliness which is Kuji—but we did not realize that our purpose would so soon ear signs of fruit. My neighbors, just across the street from my 'haunted house' are an interesting family. The mother not only has borne twelve children which would seem to be enough of a job, but to feed and clothe them she peddles fish all day in two baskets swung on a pole across her shoulder. The father makes a little money raising and selling a pig or two and then drinks it all up. The third from the smallest child is in kindergarten—and the second from the eldest boy, a fine lad of seventeen, works with the electric company. He was over in the new building fixing a switch and said, "After seeing your lovely building I have determined we must fix our house—it is more important to have a nice place to live than to save money. I want my father to come and see your nice floors and all, and maybe he will give up drinking so that we can have a better home. Where did you get this flooring and could we get some too?"

There are still over twelve thousand villages in Japan where no Christian work is being done, so the day of the pioneer missionary need not be over. In this county of which Kuji is the county-seat, there are twenty-two villages and a population of about ninety thousand and ours is the only Christian work.

Our purpose is to make Kuji the center and to work out from here into the many villages. This prefecture of Iwate is the largest and poorest in Japan (and only two Protestant missionaries in the whole prefecture) and this county the poorest and most backward in the prefecture, so the needs and opportunities for service are great. We have work started in three villages, in two of which we rent rooms in farmhouses and have Sunday School (though not on Sunday), and in one village we have rented a small house and opened a little day nursery of thirty children (training a village girl for the work), and a Sunday School. To the Sunday school about one hundred children come, completely crowding the little house—and of course this number is only possible because all sit on the floor. They all come early for even the older children are fascinated by the few toys, dolls and picture books we have taken out for the little children. In this place we were asked by the village chief to open a Busy Season day nursery, which we were glad to do. This means a week of tending to children while whole families work from early till late transplanting rice.

Perhaps we could take 'Building' as our motto. For in spite of innumerable difficulties we are looking forward to

II. "To Sow the Seeds, To Try to Follow up on Results" | 75

continue building. My own residence with a dormitory wing for an increasing staff, and country girls in training is yet to be started. Then as the way opens we want to erect more buildings to meet community needs for more abundant life and to do more in the way of wholesome recreation and public health, in all fulfilling our purpose of building character and the Kingdom of God.

Thomasine Allen

[Document 2]

BISHOP'S HOUSE
9 MOTOKAJI-CHO
SENDAI, JAPAN

June 1, 1940.

Dear 'Tommy'

Many things have happened since that short but memorable visit to Kuji. When I returned home from Noshiro last Monday afternoon, I received a telephone message from Tokyo saying that Dorothy Hittle was much worse and would probably only live a few days. Willie and I left by the 4.30 express Tuesday morning and found when we arrived that that was just the moment that Dorothy passed from the cares and sufferings of this world into the joys and peace of Paradise. The services In St. Luke's Chapel on Thursday and here in Sendai yesterday were a beautiful tribute to her wonderful life of courageous service for the Master. In her death, the mission has sustained a great loss but we rejoice in the triumph of her faith. She was a faithful soldier and servant of her Master to the very end of her earthly life and I feel that now she is experiencing great delight in an even more perfect service in the presence of her Master.

Tommy, I cannot begin to tell you what that visit to Kuji meant to me. I am afraid I was so physically weary when I arrived that I had little to give but I certainly received much inspiration from what I saw of your wonderful work, which I am sure is destined to become one of the outstanding pieces of rural evangelism in Japan. The building is a miracle. In its simplicity and beauty it reveals the character of Jesus. As I walked through it, I could see Him standing there in the midst of that drab village stitching out His loving arms to bless all who enter its doors. The plan and workmanship are excellent, and no one knows better than I, what it cost in thought, prayer and physical energy to erect. Others may have given the money to make it possible, but you and Obara San have put something of your own lives into it. I think this is what I was conscious of more than anything else. Your love and devotion have been wrought into the building and that is why it is so beautiful.

Then too, in spite of the depressing atmosphere of the present days, it is most inspiring to see two people who refuse to have their vision destroyed, and who dare to attempt great things for Christ. You are both marching in the right direction and you can be sure that just ahead of you, the Christ goes forward leading you on to even greater adventures for Him and His Church. There will be those who will try to pull you back, but Christ is not among them. He is out there in those hovels and off in those villages among the hills preparing the way for you and Obara San. You have no need for discouragement or doubt. You will need physical and spiritual endurance to realize your vision, but these will not be lacking. Christ will give you the strength and the power

II. "To Sow the Seeds, To Try to Follow up on Results" | 77

needed in such pioneer work, but remember that He expects you both, to conserve your energy and take every opportunity to replenish your inspiration and hope. You must come away from time to time to gather new strength for your work.

I wish that I could write at greater length, but I wanted to get this note off to you today and so keep my promise to write before the week passes.

I am leaving for Morioka and Kamaishi this morning and because you have lived and worked in both places, you will be much in my mind on this trip.

God bless you in everything that you are doing and fill you full of radiant hope and joy.

With affectionate regards and my thanks for all your kindness to me,

I am

Sincerely yours,
Norman Binsted

P.S. Please tell Obara San I was sorry not to see her again before the train pulled out but I appreciate her effort to get to the station and shall hope to see her in Kuji again next year. I think Kuji must always be included in my itinerary.

III

World War II
(1941–43)

The relationship between Japan-the US became worse day by day. Americans in Japan struggled to decide whether to stay or to return home. On 22th Feb. 1941, G. Washington's Birthday American Embassy called them together to Tokyo. The State Department suggested that it might be better for them to return to their home.

> * It was a very sad day for all of us because we didn't know what to do. If our State Department thought we ought to come home, then perhaps we should. On the other hand, there were some who thought that they might be able to help ease relations if they stayed. We didn't know what would happen to us if war came: whether we would be interned, whether we would be free, or whether we could help the Japanese or not. Each person had to decide what he himself thought best. Many went home, especially those with families, but there were some of us single people who thought that perhaps it was our duty to stay. I do not know whether we were right or wrong, but we couldn't do any more than live up to the best light we had at the time. (A. Hem., p. 74)

Even in Kuji, people became so nervous when they met Miss Allen, and sometimes they tried to avoid her. And when she was aware that police were following her, she was very worried whether her presence might have an bad influence on the Kindergarten.

CHAPTER I

❧

The Outbreak of War: Detention

On 8th Dec. 1941 Pearl Harbor Day, at five o'clock in the morning five policemen came to Miss Allen's house. They told her that she had to be interned as an enemy alien, so she should quickly get dressed and pack warm clothes; but they did not tell her what had happened, nor to where they would take her.

> * I did manage to get a little breakfast, and while the police men were out walking around the house, I thought I'd burn up a few papers that were on my desk. I was just putting the last one in the stove when a policeman came in and said, "Don't burn that; don't burn anything; you may need them." So I desisted, but I learned later that after I had been taken away, they went through my house with a fine tooth comb. Believing that I was a spy, they tried to find anything suspicious at all. But they found only the little piece of paper I had started to burn, and it happened to be a recipe for a one-egg cake!
>
> I was taken to the police station immediately and told to

82 | BUILD UP, BUILD UP, PREPARE THE ROAD!

wait there until train time. The chief of police was most kind, and he said to me, "We do not want to intern you, but these are orders from Tokyo, and we have no other choice. We do admire you; we admire the work you have been doing, and we want you to come back after the war." Then I knew that the war had started, but when I asked where it had started, he said that was a military secret which I wasn't to know. (A. Hem., pp. 74-75)

(1) Internment camp in Morioka (Dec. 1941–Mar. 1942)

The Christian Educational Center in Morioka, where Mr. & Mrs. Schreor lived with two daughters was used as the asylum in Morioka. Four French Canadian Dominican priests and six Belgian Dominican nuns joined, also.

* We were one big happy family, although happy may not be the adjective to put there; but we did have many good times in spite of our fears. These fears were very real. It was on December 21, that Mr. Gilbert was taken away. (He wrote those scenes in his book *Through the Storm* (Japan 1991, pp. 69)).We didn't know where he was, and I had no idea what they going to do to me because my work had been almost exactly the same as his. I kept waiting for knock on the door thinking I'd be taken to prison too, and I kept a bag packed for that purpose.

The government fed us, and the meals were adequate, but there was nothing fancy. I think that we suffered the most from the cold, for the stove in our room wouldn't burn, and in the room where we ate there was no fire at all. We were supposed to speak only Japanese so the guards could understand, but by using some French, some English, and some Latin, we got around the guards.

Of course, the hardest thing was not to know what was going to happen. The two children were nine and eleven, and they were about the best sports of all, even though they had no other children with whom to play, and no toys and no books. We weren't allowed outside at all unless we had permission to walk in the garden for an hour or so, but it was so cold and snowy that we stayed indoors. Physically, it wasn't bad; our biggest troubles were mental.

It was awfully hard for us to celebrate Christmas, but we did. We had the crib, we sang the hymns; Catholics and Protestants together, we kept our Christmas, but I think it was one of the hardest Christmases that I have ever had. Of course I kept thinking about Kuji, wondering what they are doing that Christmas....

After Christmas the Belgian nuns wanted to learn Japanese from me. The priest gave permission so every day we studied from the Japanese New Testament. We made chart and an outline of each book in the New Testament. They were very happy doing it. And they have often told me how much they appreciated the notebooks which we made at that time. It helped me of course, and I think it was a good thing all the way around. I feel very close to them, and whenever I go to Morioka, I always try to go out to the convent to see them. (A. Hem., pp. 76-77)

Generally speaking, the difference between Protestant and Catholic had been fairly big, so that they could never get along

84   BUILD UP, BUILD UP, PREPARE THE ROAD!

well each other, especially in daily life. But in the asylum, it was different. Fifteen Christians had deepened their faith and mutual understanding. They had to help one another. Miss Allen thought that one of the advantages living together was that it helped to understand each other. She had decorated a statue of the Virgin Mary and a rosary on the chest of her bed room in the Allen memorial house in Kuji.

(2) Internment camp in Sendai (Mar.–Dec., 1942)

In March of 1942 the Belgian nuns were permitted to return to their convent, and Miss Allen, Mrs. Schroer with two daughters, and five Dominican priests were moved to Sendai. In September, the Swedish liner, *Gripsholm* made its first trip to exchange interned private citizens from the two countries. Again Miss Allen had to decide whether to stay in Japan or to go back to the States.

> * I just didn't see my way clear to go on the first exchange ship. Our board had said in beginning that it was up to us out here to decide; that they would stand by us if we stayed, and they would stand by us if we left. Each one should determine himself what was the best thing to do, and so I didn't go on that first exchange ship.... I and Miss Bixby (two women who were interned with thirty Roman Catholic priests) tried to do as much as we could of so-called women's work for everybody. I remember that I was doing the washing one time and had a good many of the white Dominican socks

III. World War II | 85

in my laundry. One of the priests came along and said, "Oh, Miss Allen, you're doing all this work and not getting any merit as they saw it!" I tried to tell him that was not doing it for merit as they saw it.

Months later I was asked how I looked so well when we had suffered for insufficient and inadequate food, and my reply was that man did not live by bread alone. What should we have done without this food for the inner man? ....

There was a candle of kindness with most of our policemen. I remember that the chief of police in Kuji, after he told me that I would have to be interned, turned to the policeman who was to take me to Morioka and said, "Don't walk by Miss Allen on the street. Don't sit a seat beside her seats. Don't do anything to embarrass her."

One time in Sendai several girls came with flowers which they wanted to give us. They were girls from the Christian schools, Miyagi and Shokei. They wanted to show us that they sympathized with us and that they loved us in spite of the war. The guard turned them away, but they came back several times. Finally, seeing that they couldn't get in, some of them came to a house near the one in which we were interned, and they spent one whole evening singing and playing the little organ that they had moved outdoors so we could hear it. I think that evening of music was one of most touching things that happened during the whole time.

Another time a little note was found which read, "Do not be discouraged. We are becoming stronger Christians because you are there suffering for us." I don't know who wrote it, but it was meant for all of us.

The priests were allowed to say masses in the church next door, and Japanese Catholics had the opportunity to come for the early morning mass at five o'clock. Attending the services, Miss Allen was able to get great spiritual help. The policemen seldom inspected at that hour. One early morning Takeshi Yahaba visited her and asked her permission to marry Miss Kuni Ohara (A. Hem., p. 78)

(3) Internment Camp in Tokyo (Dec., 1942–Sept., 1943)

In 1942, the laws against enemy aliens were severely enforced, and the internees who were in Sendai, in Hiroshima, and in Nagasaki were sent to the detention camp in Tokyo. It was a large camp accommodating more than 130 foreigners. Miss Allen met many old friends and learned from them that the living conditions of the people were getting worse day by day throughout Japan. One of them told her that the tension of keeping loyalty and friendship for both nations at war was getting almost unbearable. "It was like a chronic headache; if you turned to the right, one side ached, and if you turned to the left the other side started. When we were interned, it was a great relief to us."

The internees celebrated Christmas of 1942 peacefully. And preparing for the coming year, the life of this large group of internees was reorganized to work in captivity. Meanwhile, the United States Army recovering from the shock of Pearl Harbor, strongly made a counterattack on the Japanese Army. Of course internees in the camp didn't know anything about it.

Here is a letter from Miss Allen to her sister Margret;

III. World War II 87

[Report 6]

Letter from internment camp

Addressee: Mrs. W. W. Bartlett, 226, Hamilton Ave.,
Westerville, Ohio, U. S. A.
See Des Prisonniers de Guerre
Sumire Jo Gakuin, Denenchofu 3419,
1 Chome, Tamagawa, Setagaya Ku, Tokyo.
April, 10, 1943

Dearest Home-folks;

So glad to receive your letter last fall. It was good of you to take the chance and write even the circumstances were against you.

I am with many friends in this internment camp and we are nicely treated so please do not worry. Will you please notify the Board and all other friends of my safety and in good health.

Red Cross gifts helped to make Christmas and succeeding days happier.

All thanks to them.

Cherry trees are bursting into bloom giving promise of spring and perhaps an opportunity of seeing you are so much longer.

Lovingly,
Allen

Post marked "Tokyo Nippon 16. 6 '42"

Examined by U.S.A. 131

In the camp, people were suffering from inconvenience and hunger. One day a Japanese guard came back from shopping, and said "you are all getting so thin, but we have not much for you to eat. All Japanese people are troubled by a lack of food." He had only one basket of vegetables for the 130 internees. So Miss Allen determined to "evacuate" from Japan. She was sure that because of her friendship with Japanese she had to leave this country which was suffering from starvation.

In September, it was decided that the Swedish liner *Gripsholm* would set sail from N.Y. to Goa (a Portuguese colony), where the Japanese and the people of allied nations would be exchanged. It was the last opportunity for interned civilians to leave Japan. She entrusted her tasks entirely to Kuni and Takashi who came to Tokyo to say "Good bye", and embarked on the Japanese liner *Teiwa Maru*.

CHAPTER 2

"We are free here, and we can talk"

(1) Aboard the *Gripsholm*

On September 14, 1943, after all the internees went aboard, the *Teiwa Maru* left from Yokohama. On October 15, when they reached Goa, the *Gripsholm* was already docked in the harbor. The exchange was made on the 19th October, 1,345 people on the *Teiwa maru* were exchanged with 1,525 people on the *Gripsholm*. In the salon of the *Gripsholm* the people saw the world of America. Everything was prepared for them, plenty of food; sandwiches, fruits, cakes, fresh milk. There were not only their bedrooms and bathrooms, but also a beauty salon and a theater were available.

From Goa the *Gripsholm* sailed across the Indian Ocean to Port Elizabeth on the Cape of Good Hope. From Port Elizabeth, she set a course through the Atlantic for the port of Rio de Janeiro.

* That was an experience I can never forget! The American officer lent us money to go shopping in Port Elizabeth; we could borrow fifteen dollars if we didn't have any money with us when we disembarked, there was a whole big auditorium just filled with people waiting to welcome the "Mercy Ship" (that's what the *Gripsholm* was called), and thy divided up so that everyone on our ship could be entertained in some home. The people from Port Elizabeth certainly were hospitable, and we could do anything we wanted to do during this short time that we were ashore.

An old friend of mine living there heard in some way that I was on the boat and came down to meet the ship. When he asked, "What is the very first thing you want to do?" I replied, "I want a chocolate ice cream soda." So we went to a very lovely place, and I had a wonderful chocolate ice cream soda. Then he asked, "What do you want to do next?" and I said, "I want to have a banana split." Before he got through with me, my friend thought that he probably would never fill me up. (A. Hem., p. 82)

In the middle of November, she started to sail from Rio de Janeiro to New York. They were getting closer to their destination, and day by day the excitement of the passengers mounted. On December 1, when the *Gripsholm* entered New York port, it was dawn, so there was nobody to meet them on the wharf. Instead, there were government officials and intelligence men to inspect the passengers quite thoroughly and a medical quarantine was done one by one. Miss Allen was waiting impatiently and anxiously to meet her mother. The relatives and friends of the passengers had to wait in the Prince George Hotel. She said, "It really was a very remarkable evening, one that has to be imagined rather than explained."

When she was allowed to go to the Prince George, she could not find her mother; her sister Marguerite Bartlett was standing alone. Their mother Lola Waggoner Allen had died on 15 November, just two weeks earlier.

A Welcome reception was held for all of the missionaries who had returned on the *Gripsholm*. Miss Allen was chosen to make a speech representing the group. In memory of her beloved mother, she rose to speak.

* High on a mountain overlooking Rio there is a beautiful statue of Christ holding out His hands in loving invitation. As our ship sailed past this on our way to freedom, there was a lower hill for a brief time blotted out the higher one; but soon the perspective changed, and we could see that in its true proportion, the hill which had loomed so large was really very small. But the statue on the mountain was high and visible to the last, and the arms outstretched in the distance made it appear as a cross. "And I, if I be lifted up from the earth will draw all men unto me." May the time come when the lower hill of war will be passed and the cross on the mountain top be seen again as the outstretched arms of our Master invite both East and West," Come unto me all ye that labor and are heavy laden; and I will give you rest," (A. Hem., p. 85)

(2) Activities in the United States

The United States to where Miss Allen came back was not the same nation as twenty eight years earlier. There was steel hostility toward Japan and Japanese, but she found the real freedom and justice living in the people's hearts.

> * We had had to be careful for so long that I could not get used to the idea that once we were on the *Gripsholm*, we were really and truly free. I seem to have always considered myself a prisoner of war. Just before reaching New York, I told one of the officers that I would stay in New York for three weeks and then go to Indiana. When he said, "Fine, but why do you think you have to tell me?" He laughed and said, "Don't you know you'll be in America. You don't have report to anyone." It was in a way, my first feeling of what democracy is. Again, I was being entertained at a dinner in a restaurant, and the people were freely discussing the war and coming of peace, when I cautioned, "Don't talk so loud. People at the next table can hear you." But my hosts responded, "Well, so what? This is America; we're free here, and we can talk!" It was long time before I really and truly felt liberated. (A. Hem., p. 85)

Miss Allen returned to Franklin to visit old friends of her childhood, who always had been helping her financially and spiritually; Mrs. M. E. Crowell, Mr. and Mrs. Robert A. Todd etc. The *Franklin Evening Star*, which was run by the Todds, had reported the progress of the *Gripsholm*. They asked her "Which country do you consider as your home?" "That's what the FBI asked me on the ship. Of course, I am American." She began to speak about her experience in Japan at the First Baptist Church in Franklin. Continuously, under the auspices of the American Baptist Foreign Mission Society, she went around the nation, giving lectures on her experiences in Japan, telling how Japanese were friendly and gentle in this war time.

* The FBI knew what I was saying ;they were on the job, all right, but they never interfered—not once. There were so few of us who had been interned in Japan during the war years that I felt it was my calling (if you want to put it that way), to talk about Japan and let people know firsthand what some of our experiences were.

At beginning of my speech I nearly always said that everyone knew the dark side of Japan; they could see it in the newspapers, and they could hear it from other people. But there were only a few who could tell them of the better side of Japan during the war from their own experience. And so in all of my talks I never tried to minimize the bad parts; but I did try to emphasize the fact that there were kind people, even among the guards of the internment camps, and that there was a better side to the Japanese than what we saw in the papers. Many, many people used to thank me with tears in their eyes for telling them that there was another Japan. Of course, not everyone felt that way; many people came to talks expecting to hear all about horrible atrocities. We were treated nicely in all of the camps in which I was interned, and I only told of my own experiences. We were hungry and

94 | BUILD UP, BUILD UP, PREPARE THE ROAD!

cold most of the time, but as far as atrocities or anything like that, there were none. I'm sure that most of the church people were glad to know that there was this better side to Japan and to our internment. (A. Hem., pp. 85–86)

[Report 7]

New York, Dec. 9, 1943

Dear Friends:

"Little Yeller cage bird preens his wings,
And mounts his perch and sings and sings.
He feels his cage but I guess he 'low
He'll take what comes and sing anyhow.
And he isn't by himself in date
No, he isn't by himself in dat."

Which I believe expresses what we all tried to practice during the long months of confinement, and I can even say years, as I was taken at the very beginning of the war, Dec. 8, 1941. Since I have been absolutely out off from the outside world for these last two years, not receiving any mail either foreign or domestic, (and practically no opportunity of seeing any Japanese people beside policeman,) perhaps you would like to know a bit of my history in the four different camps of which I was an inmate.

I was awakened at 5:30 by six policemen: "Pack your bedding, washbasin, and warm clothes and be ready to leave in an hour", they said. So with these police friends swarming over my little Japanese house (for I had not yet moved into my new home which was just being completed) I managed to dress while they packed for me. I was then taken to the police station to wait for my train as I was by that time told

III. World War II   95

that I was to be interned in Morioka with a family I knew well. The Chief of Police called me into his room and said, "We have the greatest respect for you and your work and this is not a personal matter. We want you to come back". Then turning to the policeman who was to escort me, he said, "Wear civilian clothes, do not talk with Miss Allen nor embarrass her in any way—let it be as the she ware travelling alone."

In Morioka I was taken to the house of Mr. and Mrs. Schroer and their two children, 9 and 13 years of age. The other "guests" were four young Dominican fathers (Canadians) and a few days later we 'welcomed' six Dominican nuns (Belgians) which necessitated all of us moving from the residence into the kindergarten building next door. The day after the Sisters came, Mr. Schroer was suddenly taken to the police station for investigation, and I was destined not to see him again till the two trips of the *Gripsholm* landed us on American soil. No words of mine can adequately describe to you the terror of those first few months—where was Mr. Schroer? For we could not get any information where and why was his Japanese co-worker taken? Would I be taken next and where and why? Were my Japanese co-workers suffering because of their connection with me? What would the next knock on the door mean? But 'knock' is figurative for now it was the home of officialdom and a knock was not necessary. These questions and many more kept Mrs. Schroer and me awake night after night as we lay in bed together, for in the daytime we had to keep up for the sake of the others who had their own like problems. At first our mental distress was so uppermost the physical inconveniences were quite secondary—the inconvenience of ten of us living in the large circle room of the kindergarten. The Kindergarten children had all been to send home early on the 19th, just before their Christmas in order to occupy the building for internees. "But when is our Christmas?" they asked bewilderedly as they took all of their possessions and left for home after song and prayer with their teacher.

Later in Tokyo where my space was about 6 feet by 3, I was to look back with a bit of longing at this rattling about in the large room. A little stove in the center of the room, that mostly smoked, left much to be desired in the way of heating—but hot water bottles used day and night made life a bit more comfortable. The stove in the room of the priests across the hall burned batter so when the pathway seemed clear of policemen we would surreptitiously get some hot water from their stove. Tea cups at meal time solved the question of keeping our hands a bit warm while eating. We ate our meals in the kitchen with watchmen at an adjoining table and they insist us on speaking only Japanese. We generally spoke Japanese, but between us we spoke English, French and Latin. We were under constant surveillance. How COULD we face Christmas—the time of peace, goodwill, joy and happiness! The words "Fear not", rang out with new emphasis so with a bit more courage in our hearts we asked police permission to have the Fathers come into our room. Gathered around the Bethlehem crèche which the two children and Sisters had put up, the Fathers in their pure white Dominican robes, and the Sisters in their white habits and veils, Mrs. Schroer, the children and I sang the old, old Christmas hymns. We invited the police in and sang some songs in Japanese. The body was there but the heart was in Kuji celebrating Christmas with all my children there, the

III. World War II   97

program we had practiced together. In this way passed my first Christmas in an internment camp.

At the end of March we were suddenly told that the Belgian nuns could return to their convent the next day. It was a sad parting—for common sorrows, anxiety, joys, laughter and tears and faith in God and His leading had welded our diversity into unity and to say goodbye to them after singing and kneeling in benediction was a re-opening of old wounds—and the place was well watered with the tears of us all. As soon as they left we were told that we must pack immediately with lists of everything, and be ready to leave at 8 the next morning for Sendai. The six of us and the two children were taken by four police to a former mission residence where five other priests, two lay brothers and six of our Protestant group awaited us. Here it took a lot of patience for five of us to be sleeping on the floor of the living room, where in happier days we had sat in easy chairs and had had carefree hours. Here began a real family life, all twenty of us working, worshipping, playing and studying together. Here I had my first contact with the outside world when the Swiss delegate visited us and I learned of Tokyo friends—how most of them were free! After about two months we were taken to the main Sendai camp in the Catholic compound, as the exchange ship was taking many of our number and we were being reorganized. Here for the first time I was with a member of our Baptist Family—Alice Bixby, and was with her and this larger group for about three weeks, when twenty left to be evacuated. Another goodbye had to be said as in the darkness our friends passed thru the gate beyond which we could not step foot, and out into eventual freedom, leaving Miss Porter, a young missionary who had only been out a year and should have been on the evacuation list; an English couple—who went a few weeks later and me with about 30 young Fathers and lay brothers. And then began a new phase of life. With one exception I was the oldest member of the group and so in many ways tried to serve as a mother to my huge family of 'sons'. The Catholic Church adjoined our house and was open to us from 5 to 6 in the morning as well as an hour in the afternoon. I never missed a morning going from 5 to 6 and this quiet worship time as well as the occasional afternoon service meant everything to me. Months later I was asked how I looked so well when we had suffered from insufficient and inadequate food and my reply was that man did not live by bread alone. What should we have done without this food for the inner man!

At the end of August we were all called into the office and told that we must leave for America in three days. I had never applied for evacuation as I felt I wanted to stand by my little flock and new work in Kuji as long as possible—but now it was taken out of my hands. They telephoned for two of my co-workers to come down to say goodbye—but the awfulness of that day after our short interview, I prefer to forget! When we each had our suitcases packed and all of our things given away and were just about ready to leave for the train, we were again called in and told that the ship was postponed. It turned out to be postponed for just a year.

In October our "Woman's Society" of two was rein-forced by the arrival of five Franciscan Sisters from Sapporo and we welcomed them into our happy congenial family. But good times, in spite of the ever present guards who certainly did not follow any Japanese pattern for politeness, had to come to an end on Dec. 20th this camp which had meant so much to us in laughter and in tears was broken up and we all went to Tokyo together—the men to one camp and we to the woman's camp where Mrs. Axling and Miss Meline of our Baptist group awaited us. There were about 150 of us, 100 sisters of 11 different orders, and 30 Protestants. We were again in a Catholic institution which had a beautiful chapel—a real refuge in a time of distress. And so life began again for me in the 4th camp, getting adjusted anew to terribly crowded conditions, new people, and new life in an institutional camp not a family one as we had had heretofore. But by that time we had learned to "take what comes and sing anyhow", and of course there were many things to sing about.

But Christmas was again a hard one. We had just arrived and lonely, this time not only for our own family and work but also for our former follow-internees, some of whom we had been with from the very beginning—and we knew they were missing us for we had truly been a happy family. However the beautiful chapel services, the pageant, the lovely Christmas touches that the Sisters with their skill in making something beautiful out of nothing could give, made it a never-to-be forgotten day. Truly we all tried to make our prison windows golden windows.

And what shall I say of the winter days without fire— only that we were thankful there was nearly always glorious sunshine and work to be done to keep us warm (for we did all the work of the camp), with bed right after early supper, hugging an earthen jar of hot water and always from our window the majestic sight of Mt. Fuji calling us to higher things—to look up and not down.

At last the much rumored and talked of ship materialized. Those living nearby were permitted to go home for a night FREE. As I lived too far away they telegraphed for two of my co-workers to come down, and then loft me alone with them for a whole day. Can you imagine what that day meant to me—a whole two years talk crowded into hours. I then learned that our work was growing and that there were agencies and persons deeply interested in our lone bit of service in the far north. And so this time when I told them goodbye the thankfulness for God's leading and protection far out-weighed the personal sorrow at parting.

High on a mountain overlooking Rio there is a beautiful statue of the Christ holding out His hands in loving invitation. As our ship sailed past this on our way to freedom there was a lower hill that for a brief time blotted out the higher, but soon the perspective changed and we could see in its true proportion the hill which had loomed so large as really small, and the statue on the mountain high, and visible to the last—but the arms outstretched in the distance appeared as a cross. "And I, if I be lifted up, will draw all men to me."

May the time come when the lower hill of war will be passed and the cross on the mountain top be seen again as the outstretched arms of our Master inviting East and West—"Come unto me all ye that are weary and heavy laden and I will give you rest".

Thomasine Allen

Every time Miss Allen spoke of her experiences in Japan at various churches throughout the United States, she had a great influence on the audience. Here is a letter from a young soldier to someone (anonymous), which was treasured in a drawer of Miss Allen's desk. We could not find whether the soldier had

III. World War II | 101

died or not, or from where he came. But we are able to see the beautiful tree grown from the tiny seed which she had planted. She wrote that an American soldier relates the most wonderful experience of his life.

[Document 3]
"I DON'T DESERVE THAT MEDAL "
A letter written by a teen-age soldier

You asked about my medal. I haven't told the story of it to anyone, and you will see why when you hear about it. I am not very proud of it and yet there isn't a thing I can do about it now, without revealing a story that would get my new friends into trouble. You may tell the story so long as my name is never attached to it. It is now two a.m. Tomorrow I go off to the battlefield. I may never get home again and I want someone to know that I don't deserve that medal. I didn't earn it.

It happened this way. I was captured by the Japanese with five of my pals. We were marched along through the jungle with bayonets in our backs. As we marched toward the Japanese camp I had to see my comrades one by one killed, mutilated, torn limb from limb. They were men with whom I had spent three years—not three years of casual friendship, either. When you live with men night and day, winter and summer; when you work with them, suffer with them, fight with them, you become attached to them more closely than you will ever become with any other men the rest of your lives. As I watched them fall I knew that within a few minutes I, too, would be killed as they had been. But, somehow, at that moment my only thought was "the sooner the better." Life for me was over. I said the 23rd Psalm. (Do you remember the time you made me come back to church for a whole afternoon to learn it because you insisted that I earn by Bible?) I said the Lord's Prayer and then I started to think things over. A good bit of the Yankee spirit stayed with me. Die I must, but I determined not to let my captor see my fear.

Trembling from head to foot, marching in mud up to my ankles, with a bayonet sticking in my back, I began to whistle the way I used to when I was a small boy and had to go through a dark street. So I whistled as loud as my trembling lips would let me. After a while, to my surprise I realized I was whistling.

> "We gather together to ask the Lord's blessing.
> He chastens and hastens His will to make known.
> The wicked oppressed, ceased then from distressing.
> Sing praises to His name, He forgets not His own."

My thoughts turned back to the many times we had sung it in Forum. You said one time you supposed that no matter where we might be the rest of our lives, if was ever heard that song we would think of Forum and our Church. Well, as I whistled it over and over I did think of the old Forum crowd, of our church, and of the various individuals in it. I realized for the first time how much the church had done for me. It had molded my character and given me the stuff to be able to take what the Army gave me and take it knowing that I was not alone, that God was with me. I thought how the church stood for eternal life. That sharp point in my back would start me on my long journey to eternity. But now I was no longer afraid.

III. World War II   103

Suddenly, from my reverie I became aware that someone had joined me in my whistling. No, it couldn't be, but it was—my Japanese captor! He, too, was whistling the hymn. Soon we broke into words, he in Japanese, I in English. "The wicked oppressing, cease then from distressing.... He forgets not His own." One after another were the hymns we whistled and sang as we marched through the jungle mud, with me in front and my captor in the rear, with now his gun in my back. Gradually the power of hymns made me relaxed, and must have had the same effect on him, for soon I felt his gun fall into place. And still later he caught up with me and we sang, he in Japanese, and I in English.

He had learnt I wondered if his thoughts were as mingled with mine. Hero we were marching along, lifting our hearts in unison in Christian praise to a Christian God of peace, and yet I was being led to the slaughterhouse by him. I was interrupted in my thinking by his words in perfect English: "I never cease to wonder at the magnificence of Christian hymns." Startled by his English, I jumped and we both laughed. Soon we were talking, I asked where did you speak English and he replied that he had gone to Christian mission schools. "Not Glory kindergarten?" I asked. "Why, I started in Glory Kindergarten." he replied. "How do you know it?" Then I told him how in Sunday school we had studied about the Congregational schools and churches. We had raised money for Glory Kindergarten and had sent over gifts for them. I spoke of the gift of the picture we sent and the letters we had back from the teachers. We remembered the picture and added that when the picture was presented he had helped to fix the flowers for the beauty corner where the picture was placed.

Then followed a conversation that is impossible to relate— one that few men have ever had with one another, when surface things are swept away and the soul stands out on top. We talked of war and how the Japanese Christians hate it; of Christianity and its power in the world; of what it would mean if people would over dare to live it; of the incomparable value of the missionaries; of Kagawa; of our own ideals—for our homes, our jobs, and our future families. And finally, at his suggestion, we knelt in the mud and prayed for suffering humanity around the world; for "the peace of God, which transcends all understanding," (Philippians 4:7) and for peace again on earth with good will toward men.

When we arose he asked if I would take him back as a prisoner to the American headquarters. He said that this was the only way he could live up to his Christianity and thus help Japan to become a Christian nation and on the way back he found in various foxholes other Japanese Christians and they, too, joined me as who walked toward the American headquarters. I shall never forget the hope and joy that came into their eyes as my Japanese friend unfolded to them, one by one, as he met them, how we found each other and why and where they were being taken. All the way back we talked of the Christian religion. You know, after being born into Christianity, I had taken its teachings for granted, I never shall again. I know now—from those Japanese friends— what Christ can moan to an individual or a nation that has lived under a hideous system of heathen gods. I know that it means the difference between Japanese atrocities and my new Japanese friends with their high Christian ideals.

We sang in English all the great universal hymns of the ages—Faith Of Our Fathers; A Mighty Fortress Is Our God;

III. World War II | 105

Load On, O King Eternal; The Church's One Foundation; Spirit of God Descend Upon My Heart.

When we neared camp, by mutual agreement, they put on poker faces and somber looks and I, gun in hand, marched with them into camp. After the war is over they will spend their lives keeping alive and spreading an over growing Christian community in Japan. So, you see, I don't deserve a medal for the most wonderful experience of my life. You surely see now why I don't want to talk about may medal.

(3) Tule Lake Relocation Camp (1945–47)

In 1945, after completing the two-year lecture tour all over the nation, Miss Allen wanted to get a position at the War Relocation Authority which was the US civilian agency, responsible for the relocation and the detention of Japanese Americans. She felt that her experience in Japan and her Japanese language skills would make her helpful to both her own government and the Japanese internees.

In the United States, the attack on Pearl Harbor on December 7, 1941, was the gravest shock to the military and political leaders. They suspected that Japan might be preparing for a full-scale attack on the West Coast. Civilians had serious concerns about the attacks to be followed, and the anti-Japanese sentiment kept getting stronger. With mounting fear and prejudice, they requested to President Franklin D. Roosevelt to watch the Japanese Americans for possible espionage activities and execute a law to allow enforced relocation of Japanese Americans. Actually at that time 114,000 Japanese American lived on the West Coast.

The President authorized bringing the Japanese Americans into internment camps with the Executive Order 9066, executed on February 19, 1942, which allowed local military commanders to designate "a military area" as "an exclusion zone", from which "any or all persons may be excluded". This power was used to declare that all the Japanese Americans be kept out from the entire Pacific coastal area. They were forced to move from their homes with one piece of baggage to the internment camps, not being told about their destination. They had to dispose of their houses, business, farms, automobiles etc.

Relocation camps were constructed in eleven inland areas which were isolated from the coast. The camp house was covered with black tar paper and the simple frame construction was without plumbing or cooking facilities of any kind. Many camps were built quickly during the summer of 1942, based on the designs used for military emergency barracks. The houses were poorly equipped, and the areas were enclosed with barbed-wire fencing and armed guards were posted day and night. Their guns were pointing to the inside of the fence, like a prison. Many of the internees were not able to bring in appropriate clothes and living necessities of life, so the very cold winter in the interior was really unbearable for them.

After applying to work for the War Relocation Center, Miss Allen was sent to Tule Lake, California. It was the largest

III. World War II | 107

and most controversial camp, with a peak population of 187,000. Initially Tule Lake Camp was very similar to other camps, but eventually it turned into a high-security Segregation Center, by martial law and was occupied by the Army.

On February 10, 1943, the American government sent out questionnaires to all of internees in an effort to separate loyal American citizens from enemy aliens supporting Japan. Particularly the important questions were "Question 27 and Question 28", which were the most difficult ones for Japanese Americans to clearly answer.

> Question 27: "Are you willing to serve in the armed forces of the United States on combat duty wherever ordered?"
>
> Question 28: "Will you swear unqualified allegiance to the United States and faithfully defend the United States from any or all attacks by foreign or domestic forces, and forswear any form of allegiance or obedience to the Japanese Emperor, or any other foreign government, power, or organization?"

The government released all who answered "yes-yes", as they indicated their loyalty to the U.S. and segregated all who answered "no-no" into the one camp as they showed loyalty to Japan. Though this plan looked simple and workable on paper, in practice there were many family dramas, conflicts, and tragedies.

When Miss Allen arrived at Tule Lake, the disloyal and radical nationalists were held there, as the other camps were

108 | BUILD UP, BUILD UP, PREPARE THE ROAD!

already closed.

In July 1944, the Congress of the United States passed the Denationalization Bill which permitted Japanese Americans to renounce their citizenship. Public hearings were held again and again from January 11 to March 17, 1945, and more than six thousand people gave up their American citizenship. But in August, the war ended with the atomic bombs, and many Japanese wanted to recover their American citizenship. Again hearings were held, and Miss Allen patiently worked to facilitate mutual understandings of both parties.

* Many of the young Japanese rebelled at the way they had been treated by some of the authorities and at the fact that, although they were American citizens, they were interned. There were many diehards among the older Japanese people, and, of course, they influenced these rebellious young folk. Those who had been educated in Japan did not speak English, of course. It took great deal of conferring with the Department of Justice, and I was able to be of some help, I felt, in explaining the American viewpoint to the Japanese and the Japanese view point to the American.

* I explained that the living conditions of camps in America were palatial compared to what we had had in Japan. They had plenty of good food to eat, heat in their homes, and schools for their children. There was even a movie theater! Through the camp post office they could send and receive mail from the outside, but we in Japan had been allowed to write only one letter in two years. The freedom that they had in going about more than impressed me. But, of course,

America was a different country and a richer country, so, in a way, they should not be compared. (A. Hem., p. 89)

Miss Allen was able to explain about the conditions in wartime Japan for the Japanese who had not any information directly from Japan. Also she had opportunities to speak at the Buddhist organization, and became close friends with people at the organization. She wrote letters to the American Christians, and they delivered clothes for newborn babies and Christmas presents for all of the 18,000 internees. She explained to a young Japanese who was wondering why such gifts were given; "You can't understand it without a Christian background. You see, there was kindness in their hearts; they wanted to do something to show the Love of Christ, and this was the one thing they could do." She had a small Bible class for young people.

* I was impressed by the Christian background in America which makes all the difference in the world. Again, we don't appreciate that blessing until it is taken away from us and we don't have it. It is something to make one pause and be thankful that he has been raised in a Christian democracy. (A. Hem., p. 90)

When Miss Allen left Tule Lake, the minister offered her some present and she was given a shabby wooden cross which was in the Union Church of the Relocation Center, as she wished. Now it is kept in Kuji kindergarten.

(4) Wartime in Kuji and Defeat (1941–45)

Even after the war, Miss Allen did not have any information about Kuji. It was not prohibited for Americans and Japanese to exchange letters privately. In 1946, Miss Allen received a letter from Father Lamars, a French Canadian Dominican priest and one of her friends of the internment days in Japan.

> * I could not find a Baptist chaplain, so I took a Catholic chaplain and we went up to Kuji. We took them some food. They welcomed us with open arms, and I was so glad to be able to see just how they were getting along. The town had been burned, not bombed, just burned; but your buildings are safe and they are being used. The Yahabas are all well. I have told them that they can write me, and I will forward the letter to you. (A. Hem., p. 91)

As soon as Miss Allen was arrested in the early morning on the day of Pearl Harbor 1941, the rumor spread through the town in an instant. "Miss Allen was a spy." "The green roofs were a signal for American Air Forces." "She has been shot in Tokyo as a spy." Frightened mothers took back their children from the kindergarten, and the new enrollment began to decline. Kuni Obara was married to Takeshi Yahaba and had a baby. With her two sisters they faced the fact that there would be nothing to eat in the house, and they were short of money for their work.

III. World War II | 111

One night, there was a knock at the door with the voice of the mailman, who delivered a postal money order from Mr. Nobechi, an evangelist, who was one of Miss Allen's good friends. He collected three or four yen from Japanese Christians, and sent it to Kuji. One day a telegram came from Viscount Shokuma Matsukata, who had supported Miss Allen's work formerly. It said to Takeshi; "Come to Tokyo immediately." Takeshi was astonished but hastened to go to Tokyo. The Matsukatas were members of a group of Christian Scientists in Tokyo, and during the year of the famine in 1931 and the tidal wave in 1933, they had contributed not only to the whole relief work, but to Miss Allen. They had especially been interested in her activities in Kuji. She greatly appreciated their help, and had maintained friendly relations with them. Takeshi had never visited their home, nor met him.

Mrs. Hemphill described it as follows:

> * At last the Matsukatas told him that they would give him 3,000 yen for the year's work, with 1,000 yen to take back with him, the rest promised later. Almost overwhelmed, Takeshi took the bills and tucked them away carefully. (Mrs. H. Hem., p. 93)

The other important friendship was with Mr. and Mrs. Merrell Vories. In 1942, when the kindergarten building was completed, the construction supervisor from the Omi Brotherhood said that the key of the new building could not be handed over to Takeshi until he paid all of the money, 1,600yen. Takeshi explained to them how necessary it was for many people who had got away from the threat of the air raid in the cities. "No! Never!" the supervisor said. Finally Takeshi visited Mr. and Mrs. Vories in Tokyo, who resigned from the Brotherhood in Omi. Just before the war, Mr. Vories was naturalized in Japan by his Japanese wife, Makiko Hitotsuyanagi, who was of noble birth. Leaving from Omi, they lived in Tokyo with her family.

> * Mr. and Mrs. Vories-Hitotsuyanagi glanced at each other and then turned to Takeshi. They explained that they had been dismissed from the Omi Brotherhood and no longer had anything to say about its policies; but just the evening before they had received a money order containing "tear money", or severance pay, and the amount was exactly 1,600 yen. They had talked about the money and decided that it was a special fund which must not be used for personal expenses, but for some particular project instead, "And maybe, just maybe, the first person who comes tomorrow will be the one who need it. Now you take this as a gift from God. It isn't a debt, and Miss Allen needn't ever pay it back; it's a gift." (Mrs. H. Hem., p. 94)

Although the rumor of the town was not correct, it was true that there were many supporters outside of Kuji. In Tule Lake, listening to the radio about the desperate situation with indiscriminate bombings on Japan, the human torpedo and the suicide corps, Miss Allen was grieving for Japanese citizens.

At last a flash of light, a mushroom cloud and black rain opened the new nuclear age, and the war came to an end.

IV

After the War
(1947–)

Following the United States Army, the Allied Forces occupied Japan and began to settle the postwar confusion. They were faced with difficult problems of political reformation on one hand, and the reconstruction of the life of people on the other. Learning from American Democracy, an amendment of the old Japanese Constitution, the reconsideration of every system and research for responsibility of the war were launched in no time.

In 1946, a New Constitution was established, and the cabinet reshuffled. The U.S. Education Mission to Japan was organized and drastically reformed not only the educational system but also national policy. Under the banner of peace and democracy, many people were assembled at the Churches, looking for new ideas for living.

The Military Government teams were formed in local centers all over Japan, with the intention to work with prefectural and local governments, and simultaneously to calm people's feelings of hostility. And so, American soldiers went everywhere in Japan. When they visited Kuji, Kuni was called from those who could not understand what US army wished to tell them. Kuni went everywhere. She became a person indispensable in this area. American soldiers were very surprised and delighted at her fluent English. During the early time of occupation, only the military personnel or citizens were permitted to live in Japan. But in 1947, Miss Allen allowed to return to Japan.

CHAPTER I

Go Back to My Home Town

Miss Allen was fifty-seven years old, when she received permission to return to Japan. She had known that in Japan everything was lacking, especially daily necessities. As to getting ready for her return, she gathered a great deal of relief material. Of course they exceeded the load limit. The friendly chaplain helped her to take them. He sent them by taking a shipment with his personal baggage. Another friend in Tokyo accepted the chaplain's baggage.

> * My friend had not bargained for so much! A soldier who was with her at the time said to her "What on earth are you going to do with all those boxes?" When my friend said she didn't know, the soldier replied, "Well, I'm in the transportation department, and I will see that they all get up to Kuji for you." And so it worked out just like that; all things were sent up to Kuji. They met such a great need because the people had been without goods for so very long. (A. Hem., p. 102)

116 | BUILD UP, BUILD UP, PREPARE THE ROAD!

In 1947, when Miss Allen reached Kuji Station, she was astonished to be welcomed warmly by the whole town. In their delightful excitement we could see the feelings mixed with their apologies from the wartime. As soon as she settled in her house, she started to visit small villages to distribute relief supplies.

> * Would that all the churches, societies, groups, and individuals who so generously gave clothing, food, supplies, and money for our needs could witness the joy and gratitude of the recipients. Life has been one continual sharing since my return; sharing with repatriates from Manchuria, sharing with Christian workers and their families, and sharing with friends far and near. A mother wrote me a letter of thanks the other day, saying that her little four-year-old boy was so happy over his "new" clothes that he got up in the middle of the night to try them on again. He was a war baby, so he had never had such fine clothes before. (A. Hem., p. 103)

The Kuji Christian center was attached to the kindergarten. Many people irrespective of age gathered there, looking for something new for their lives. They found a real American spirit, moreover they took in a breath of freedom and democracy. Defeated Japanese would learn and adopt democracy. Miss Allen thought it as a good chance to pass on the basic ideas of democracy and Christianity. It was to be her mission. She went on to work in the educational field vigorously. She got a position to teach English at the Kuji high school and opened the gospel center for young farmers.

On May 3, 1947, Miss Allen was invited to be the guest of honor with Takeshi at a celebration in a little mountain town forty miles from Kuji. The town had built its first junior high school building and held a celebration to dedicate the school. At the same time promulgation of the new Constitution was celebrated. Transportation for the guest was a crowded charcoal-burning bus, which had only one run a day.

[Report 8]

A COUNTRY TRIP

Kuji, Iwate Ken.

May 12, 1947.

The charcoal burning bus that was to take Mr. Yahaba and me forty miles to a little town tucked away in the mountains, a town that had had no direct connection with the outside world till this halting bus was installed last month, was to leave at 1:50. So in order to get in line we left home at one o'clock. Well, we waited outdoors till 4:30, most of the people squatting on the ground, and some of us finding boxes on which to sit, not daring to return home for fear our vehicle which had had an accident would come in our absence.

When I saw people getting on the other buses, climbing in the windows and hanging on at every conceivable angle I thought to myself, "I just cannot do it—I can never get on." But we had to get on for we were to give the addresses at the celebration for the adoption of the new constitution and the opening of a new school in the little mountain town.

The man who had charge of the buses—more or less—had the driver save a seat for us and told him to get us to the transfer place in time for the other bus, even though he had to use gasoline most of the uphill road. So sitting in front and holding on for dear life we climbed up and up over the worst roads imaginable. But in between bumps and bruises I managed to cast fleeting glances at the cherry and plum trees in full bloom and to think about the kindness of the people around me and of their uncomplaining way of accepting the bumps and bruises of life.

We arrived at our destination at 8:30 rather weary and worn and found that while the meetings were scheduled for the morrow about forty young people, mostly women had gathered wanting a meeting that night. There in that isolated mountain town, a real bit of old Japan, this fine group of young people was gathered in a large upper room sitting on their feet, along two sides of the long united room patiently waiting for us. And they had questions to ask! "What is American democracy? Will it work in Japan? Tell us about American women and how they function in a democracy. What can we do to help make a new Japan? What is the relation between science and religion? Tell us about Christianity. Explain your educational system." These are samples! Well we got an interest in trying to answer some of these 'little' questions that we talked till midnight quite forgetting the bruises of the ride.

The following morning was the celebration for the new constitution, a happy occasion in which I was proud to have a part in a congratulatory speech. Always there is a feeling and expression of their guilt and thankfulness for the opportunity to learn and practice democracy and to make

IV. After the War | 119

a new Japan. This was followed in the afternoon by the opening of a new school—a Junior H. S. Up to now they had had only a primary school and those who wanted a H. S. education had to go far away to boarding schools but by the new plan every new town must have a Junior H. S.

The Principal said in his address, "I know that Miss Allen's heart aches when she sees the impoverished condition of our people but we want her to know that if Japan and Germany had won this war our situation under a fascist regime would have been intolerable. We have been saved from that and now America is giving us a chance to make a new Japan and we are thankful." Then turning to me, he said, "Please thank your people and tell them that we want and need friends—we are lonely for friends." Then Yahaba and I were given each an hour in which to make religious talks. We caught the three o'clock bus, escorted by crowds of people and got home at six—so returning it only took three hours to go forty miles! (You see why we need a Jeep!)

It was a very lovely experience and the young people want us to come regularly for meetings and discussion and to teach them. This is only one of countless opportunities around us and we must not fail to enter those open doors with the only solution to the world's needs—Jesus.

Thomasine Allen

At that time, she wanted zealously to have some means of transportation, for she wished to extend her work of the Kuji center to the entire area.

* One of our missionaries once said, "We pray God to bless our work, and then when he does, we are greatly troubled." How very true! Our budgets have a way of remaining stationary while the work grows, the needs multiply, and one spends anxious hours considering ways to meet the increased opportunities. (A. Hem., p. 104)

In 1948, two prominent Baptists visited her from the United States. A good chance she thought.

* I took both of them to Karumai in one of the charcoal-burning buses. The roads between here and Karumai were simply terrible, and we hit our heads against the ceiling almost every other minute. Then the conductor said, "From now on you must be careful, for the roads will be bad!" Although we all laughed over that, my two friends felt that our greatest need was a sturdy station wagon with four-wheel drive. Nothing else would get us over the roads or, rather the lack of roads here. So from Portland, Oregon, and from Calvary Church in Washington D.C., a beautiful station wagon came to us and made it possible for us to do more extensive work in different villages. (A. Hem., p. 105)

[Report 9]
FRIENDSHIP DAY AND DAYS
Kuji, Iwate Ken.
Aug. 15, 1947.
"A Letter from Thomasine Allen"

IV. After the War | 121

Would that all the churches, societies, groups and individuals who gave clothing, food, supplies and money for our needs so generously, could witness the joy and gratitude of the recipients. On their behalf I want to say a big Thank You to each and all.

Life has been one continual sharing since returning, sharing with repatriates from Manchuria who returned with almost nothing; sharing with Christian workers and their families; sharing with friends far and near and sharing with our whole community. A mother wrote me a letter of thanks the other day saying that her little four year old boy was so happy over his 'new' clothes that he got up in the middle of the night to try them on again. He was a war baby so had never had such 'fine' clothes before. And the parents and older children were just as happy over their things too. This is typical of all the hundreds of people who have been able to help.

With a view to long range relief I went to Morioka to talk with our fine American men there on the Iwate Military Government Team on plans. Our Christian Center Free Clinic which has steadily grown, meeting a real need in this whole area, is in need of a barrack building, so we decided on a Friendship Bazaar with some of the things that were left, which would not only help the people immediately but in thus tasking a nest egg for the clinic barrack room, help in the future in a very real way. Then I conceived the very grand idea of making cookies as I wanted the people to have at least a taste of something sweet. It was a good idea but, oh, the work! To bake millions—well, thousands—about two thousand cookies in two little square pans in a little old oven over a charcoal fire—and the charcoal not good—demanded much in the way of sweat, toil and time. But it was worth it even though I do feel like taking a rest cure!

Just the day before our Friendship day, just as I was making the last cookies and pressing some of the things for the bazaar, six fine young American soldiers came to call. They were passing thru Kuji on their way back to camp and when they heard that an American woman was living here they literally ran over and were so tickled to see an American house, sit in chairs and drink coffee "made by a woman's hand", as they said and eat some homemade cookies and fudge which they had not tasted since leaving home. They were from W.Va., Ind., Ohio, Ky., and Calif. I apologized for the upset condition of my house but they said, "But It looks like home!" I'm sure their mothers would like that!

The great day came—a perfect day—about the only perfect one we have had. (This summer has brought us only rain and floods till the grain shortage will be even more acute.) And with the day came people about three thousand or more, from miles around. I served coffee and cookies and was much too popular for my comfort for with the heat from the several charcoal fires, and the people crowding on top of us, to say nothing of the sun's rays—I was truly HOT. One of the nicest things about the Friendship Day was not only the feeling of meeting needs of various kinds, but the way everyone cooperated and sought to help. It was a real Community Project! Six Japanese friends came from a town twelve hours distant just to help us; others from near-by villages and many of the Kindergarten mothers and our Sunday night inquirers' group—in all about sixty or seventy worked hard, very hard not only that day but before and after. So Friendship Day was a real success in every way.

IV. After the War | 123

Would that every day could be a real friendship day throughout the world?

And of course I cannot close this letter without saying that always clothing of any kind, new or old, for men, women and children, and food are always more than welcome. Many of you have been sending 11 lb. boxes and they have been so wonderful to receive. (One came today.) One came recently addressed to my little three year old Junko Yahaba and she was so proud and happy. Some candy in it seemed to meet her immediate desire! I wish I could tell each of you just whore your things were being used but please know that everything given to me is being used to good advantage and is promoting many real Friendship Days.

With a THANK YOU from each of the recipients thru
Thomasine Allen

Under the occupation, American missionaries lived an ambiguous life in Japan, not being entitled to the privileges accorded military and civilian personnel of official states. But they were American citizens.

* One day I was riding on the military train as a guest of the American government. I had gone down to Tokyo and was coming back, and this was the best way to travel. The other trains were just awful, and you could scarcely get on them, anyway. I considered that I was an American citizen, that in many ways I was working under the Democracy, and my own government would be glad for me to ride on their military trains. So I got on, but naturally I didn't have any

money. I wondered how I was ever going to get anything to eat because the dining car which served the soldiers and officers accepted only military coin. So I thought, "Well, I'll just have to go without food for two or three meals until I get back home to Kuji."

Early the next morning everybody else was going in for breakfast, and the Japanese car boy asked, "Aren't you going in to breakfast?" "No, I'm not," I replied, "I don't have any military money." "Oh," he said, "We have such a nice steward, I'm sure he'll do something about it." "Oh, no, please don't do anything about it," I begged. But he came back after a while and said, "You're a missionary, aren't you?" When I said "Yes," he continued, "The steward says for you to come right on in; you can eat all you want, and it won't cost you a thing." Well, I thought that was lovely, although I was quite hesitant about doing it; but he insisted, so I went, and I thanked the steward very warmly. I thought perhaps I'd better eat enough breakfast to last me the rest of the day, because I didn't know when I'd get any more food, so I ate a big breakfast and thanked him again.

When I went back to my seat I heard someone call "Miss Allen, what are you doing here?" I wondered what was going to happen to me, but here was one of the officers from the military government in Morioka. I told him, "You've the answer to a maiden's prayer, for I'd like to borrow a dollar to pay for my breakfast and to buy lunch before I get back to Kuji." "All pay you back." He had been a guest in my home, and said, "All right, but keep the dollar, I've been over to your house and I'll be coming again."

So I took the money and went back into the dining car at noon and offered to pay for my breakfast and buy some lunch, telling the steward, "I've got some money now." But he said, "No, no, I won't take your money. You just keep it, and here's your lunch." So instead of having to fast the whole trip, I enjoyed two big meals and was a dollar to the good. (A. Hem., pp. 105–106)

There were two American military camps near Kuji; Misawa Air Base about five hours from Kuji, and Camp Haugen, about three hours away from Hachinohe. American soldiers and airmen visited Kuji officially at first. Before long they heard that an American missionary lived in Kuji in an American home, to their surprise, and they used to visit Miss Allen. The priests of the churches in the camp came to visit her, and supported her both financially and spiritually. The ladies' club of a church in Misawa Air Base was able to make a close association with the mother's club of Kuji kindergarten. Before long, the two clubs were communicating with each other and having an exchange picnic once a year. This continued for more than thirty years.

* One time when quite a group came, I happened to be ironing, and I had things strewn over the house. When I apologized for the way the house looked, they said, "Oh, but it looks just like home!" I think the mothers would be pleased to know that their sons felt right at home in my home! (A. Hem., p. 145)

[Note 1]

Kuji kindergarten

"Get up Shige Chan or you will be late for kindergarten," called her mother. The little four and a half year old girl crawled out of her 'futon' (bed) and began dressing while mother started to change the bedroom into a living and dining room. This is easily done in a Japanese house for the 'beds' can be put any place as they consist of 'futon' of flexible cotton mattresses about two or three inches thick. These are folded up and put in a specially built in closet during the day, then laid on the floor of thick mats (not hard wood floor like ours) at night and the beds made up.

Shige Chan's mother folded up the futons and after sweeping, presto, the bedroom was a nice living room. Then a little round lacquer table with folding legs was set up and presto, the living room became a dining room. Shige Chan sat with her feet folded behind her—chairs are not used on the matted floors (tatami)—and Mother brought in bowls of rice and soup and some pickled plums. Then the little girl folded her hands as they did at kindergarten and said, "Thank you" to the Heavenly Father, and taking her little chopsticks ate her good breakfast. Mother then fixed Shige Chan's lunch, putting rice in an oblong aluminum box which had compartments for vegetables or fish, and pickles. She put the box in the child's kindergarten bag, put some nose paper in her apron pocket and started here off to the place where one of the kindergarten teachers was waiting to take the children of that neighborhood on the long walk to the kindergarten.

IV. After the War

127

The last part of the trip they took the short cut thru the rice fields and had to walk carefully on the narrow path as there was water on both sides for the rice plants. It was fun to walk there and see your reflection in the water and see the men and women with their big straw hats bending over almost double, wading in the water and mud, tending to the plants which provide their daily living.

Shige Chan and her playmates greet the other kindergarten teachers who are waiting, with a bow and "Ohao Gozaimasu" (Good Morning). Then they take off their shoes, some wearing "geta"—wooden clogs—and some shoes, and put them in the built in "geta" boxes on either side of the cement entrance. Each child has its own box. Shige Chan knows her the day's activities.

In the morning service, children have their 'processional' as a quiet march is played by Miss Allen. The big room is beautiful, artistic and worshipful—the floors polished wood—great windows on either side so it seems as if the whole side is glass and sunshine—two lovely large pictures, one by Margaret Terrant and the other Christ and the Children, in blue and white harmonize with the blue window curtains and make the room worshipful. As we only have fifty little chairs and eighty children we do not use the chairs at all but have the children sit on the floor with their feet behind them. They sit quietly and reverently thru the quiet music, the prayer, hymn, and morning greeting song. Then the piano leads them into all sorts of rhythms and musical games and songs which they love. And of course there are stories, picture books, molding with clay, paper folding, drawing, playing with blocks etc. So Shige Chan is very busy. All have worked so hard they are more than ready

128 | BUILD UP, BUILD UP, PREPARE THE ROAD!

for the morning 'oyatsu' (snack) refreshments. L.A.R.A. had now provided us with milk so some mothers come every day to mix the powder, heat the milk and put it in little aluminum bowls which also came from American friends. The children all sit in a big circle and not one touches her bowl till all are served and the "Thank the Heavenly Father" song sung. Then all start and how they love it! Then all have each finished they bow and say, "Gochiso sama" (we have had a feast), and each carries his bowl to the kitchen as a march is played. Then more play on the slide and swings, sand box, bars etc. till lunch time.

At this time the children meet in respective class rooms around tables and open their little lunch boxes. How they love this hour!

Again with folded hands, the song blessing and then everyone 'falls to' with a vengeance and the little chopsticks fairly fly from box to mouth. A bit more of quiet play and the kindergarten day is over about two o'clock. The good bye song is sung, many bows of farewell made, shoes or "geta" are put on and the long trek back home with other playmates and the teacher started. (Other teachers remain to do all the cleaning.)

Shige Chan is a real comfort to her mother. She, her mother and father lived in Hiroshima where her father worked in the city office. Shige Chan and her mother were in the country just outside the city when the atomic bomb was dropped that fateful Aug. day. The mother knew that something dreadful had happen and walked into the dead city looking for her husband. Finally locating the place where the city office had been she found him living but badly burned. Someway she got him to the country where

IV. After the War | 129

after a few days he died.

Shige Chan and her mother then took the long trip to Kuji, the former home. The mother's heart is sad but she is finding a new joy in coming to our Sunday night services and mingling with our group of Christians. She is studying the Bible and loves to sing the hymns. She wants to learn more of the Jesus whom Shige Chan loves, for she is beginning to realize that it is only Christianity that can make this world a world of peace and safe from the dreadful experience she and so many others passed thru. Hiroshima—Kuji were—far, far apart, at different side of the island but bound together in Shige Chan.

CHAPTER 2

To Build and To Plant (1948–49)

> See, today I appoint you
> Over nations and kingdoms
> To uproot and tear down,
> To destroy and overthrow,
> To build and plant. (Jeremiah 1: 9–10)

I found two verbs in the first chapter of Jeremiah [RSV] which came to me with new force. The tenth verse called Jeremiah "to pluck up and to break down, to destroy and to overthrow, to build and plant. How profound! What must we build? Character? Church? Christian community? Kingdom of God? What shall we plant, and where? The land must be prepared, and the means must be found. These two little commands include everything. We must start where we are and work our own answers in the framework of our own lives. No matter how many fine blueprints there are for programs and policies, it often comes to the individual to decide in the end, and yet that is not the entire answer, either. (A. Hem., p. 107)

IV. After the War   131

Thirty three years had gone by since Miss Allen came to Japan and ten years passed since she had moved to Kuji. The War time passed, and Japan was returning to normal. The economic climate was developing, and the life of the cities was setting down gradually. However, in the rural areas, the standard of life was able to improve, but very slowly. It seemed to Miss Allen, the time to look ahead, for there were several assets upon which the future work could be built.

First of all, Miss Allen was trusted and loved by the conservative people in this area. Because they knew that during the war Miss Allen had not left Kuji until she was interned and the Yahabas also maintained the kindergarten in spite of their indifference. The people might change slowly, and they could listen to what she said about the love of God. There was no question as to her ability to direct the Center, for not only had their faith been tried and proven, they had brought their practical gifts to the work, as well. "Kuni does the planning, Takeshi does the executing, and I do the worrying."

Miss Allen was always worried about how she could collect contributions. Through widely open gates, many people gathered at the Center; peasants, fishermen, shopkeepers, and businessmen, young and old. New developments cost money. Fortunately the Center had one other asset, Miss Allen's gifts; a sense of humor and her powerful writing. She wrote letters to subscribers and friends to report expressing her gratitude. An old postman said that even when she was old, she walked with a limp to mail letters almost every day.

Once she had a chance to speak to a group of American women in Tokyo, her old friend said, "When Miss Allen gives a lecture, leave the rent money at home!"

Another friend wrote that she made a will to give her inheritance to Kuji. Miss Allen wrote briefly; "Oh good! When are you going to die?"

(1) The Farmer's Gospel School (March 1948–March 1962)

Kuji Center opened the Farmer's Gospel School with the motto of "Spirit of three loves", which are "love of God, love of man, love of soil". On the opening day twenty eight farmers enrolled in an agricultural off-season for them. Every March the school used to open. The farmers shared dormitory life and enjoyed fellowship. They listened to talks by agricultural authorities from all over Japan, and watched demonstrations of new farming and dairying practices, and they saw the results.

Hope dawned on their life in these areas. In winter, the cold wind from the ocean froze everything, and in summer, the dense fog from the ocean blocked the sunshine. The peasants worked very hard in vain.

The word, "Love of soil," caught their hearts. Of course they tried to find some means to develop agriculture in their countryside. They researched some new method suited for this land. But how would they be able to find it? Who could understand this isolated land? At the Center they learned how

IV. After the War | 133

to get away from constant poverty, the land had to be fertile; to cultivate, to improve, to plant, to raise livestock. That is dairy farming.

"Love of God, Love of man, Love of land" became their intellectual interest. Faith was also a part of the new ideas introduced at the Farmer's Gospel School, a very different kind of faith; a creator God, a God with a steadfast love for all of humanity and a purpose. This was different from the traditional belief in Japan. Some of them began to understand that there was plan for them in God's plan, a place that only He could fill.

(2) Kuji Center Clinic (July 1948–February 1963)

In 1948, the Center opened a Clinic cooperating with the Red Cross. In this area there had been neither a clinic nor a doctor. The infant mortality rate had been the highest in Japan. After the War, an idealistic Red Cross doctor, Dr. Kinoshita from Morioka, visited this area. He understood that a clinic and doctor were necessary for people's health immediately. At first he approached the government in Kuji and nearby towns, researching some sponsors for holding the clinic. But he could not find any support for his ideas. They said they had not planned to look for new funds.

Lastly Dr. Kinoshita went to talk to Miss Allen and Takeshi, who shared his concern for the health of people. Miss Allen offered the Center building for use as a clinic and agreed to cooperate with the doctors who would come to hold the clinic every two weeks from Morioka. The Red Cross doctors came regularly to Kuji clinic and cared for their patients in one of the kindergarten rooms. Thereafter they came as contract surgeons, and a few bed patients were cared for in an old Japanese house next to the Center building.

Miss Allen began to think about opening a hospital on Christian principles of care and concern for each individual patient. This new project required both much money and land, so she appealed to those who believed in Kuji activity; it was gathered and she borrowed money to make up for the shortage. Finally it was enough to start the project, but negotiations to buy the land needed much time.

> * "Why does it take so much time to get anything done?" Everything demands much, much time, and much, much unwinding of red tape. Patience is not one of my virtues— but of course, I have all of the others!" At last the building was begun, and the clinic rooms, the pharmacy, the oper- ating room, and the wards began to work. Equipment was installed, and the hospital was nearly ready for service. To the other problems was added the almost insuperable difficulty of obtaining a medical staff. Competent doctors, sympathetic to the Kuji ideals, were hard to find. (A. Hem., p. 126)

Finally a Chinese doctor decided to work in Kuji, and by 1959, the Kuji hospital began to serve the community.

(3) Kuji Church (December 1948)

Thus says the Lord
"The people who survived the sword
Found grace in the wildness...."

(Jeremiah 31:2 [RSV])

On September 26 1948, the first baptismal service was held in Kuji by the pastor of the church from the Misawa camp. Fifteen believers gathered for Christian baptism on the side of Osanai River next to the Center. On Christmas day, fourteen believers were baptized.

> * From seven in the evening till after midnight on Christmas Eve, we listened to the stories and confessions of faith of the fourteen to be baptized. They were so thrilling; it made us forget the time as each person described his struggles and victory in detail. One disillusioned ex-soldier told how he had turned to Buddhism to find the answer to his problem, but he found it not; then he had turned to the study of Communism, but the answer was not there; but he did find what he is seeking in Jesus. A war widow, a young woman who had lost her husband in the bombing at Hiroshima, had returned with her baby to Kuji, her former home; but in her sorrow she had found peace in Jesus. Christianity was something new, real, and challenging to each one, and it made some of us older ones feel very humble indeed. (A. Hem., p. 110)

On the same Christmas day, the church was organized with more than twenty nine believers. (A number of believers were the one of requirement as a church) On Sunday morning they held Sunday service in the library of the Center building, where a simple wooden cross from the Union Church of Tule Lake was hung.

In October 1940, the Japanese government collected the Protestant churches and organized them into a Kyodan, the "United Church of Christ" in Japan. After the War, it wasn't dissolved and was retained as a system to unify all Protestant Christians and Churches. In 1948, it made up the rules of church government and established standards for the admission of church bodies with several requirements, and for the licensing and the ordination of pastors. Furthermore, the churches were classified by several ranks according to the requirements.

In 1948, as Kuji Center had twenty nine believers, applied to "the Kyodan", the United Church of Christ, for the admission of Kuji Church. However there were two difficulties; the qualification for a pastor and the problems between the Baptist Church and the United Church of Christ.

> The rule of church government, drawn up in 1948, established standards for the admission of church bodies and for the licensing and ordination of pastors. Several types of church bodies were recognized, and requirements were established for their classification.

IV. After the War | 137

According to the rules, the United Church of Christ affiliated Kuji Church with an Evangelism station, not a Church. The Kuji Church decided against this affiliation of the United Church and made plans for congregational ordination. On December 8, 1951, Takeshi was ordained. Four Baptist missionaries, serving as delegates from their churches, and an American Army Chaplain from Misawa performed the service of ordination on behalf of the congregation.

* The church was present in farmer's homes, in kindergarten opening exercises, at hospital bedsides, and in the earnest after midnight conversation of two or three Christians." (A. Hem., p. 117)

[Report 10]

NEARER OUR GOAL

Christmas 1948

I heard a bird sing
In the dark of December
A magical thing and sweet to remember
"We are nearer to spring
Than we were in September,"
I heard a bird sing
On the darkness of December.

And we too are nearer in December our goal of extending the Kingdom of God to this dark, backward district, the most backward county in Japan, than we were in September. For not only has the Christmas season brought its beautiful opportunities to tell the story of Love to hundreds people, old and young, in story, pageant, song and candle service in the many worship programs from Dec. 19th to 31st, but fourteen men and women were baptized in the little river which is almost in our backyard, on Christmas Day and these with the fifteen baptized in Sept. organized the First Church in Kuji. So we feel a real advance step has been taken.

As opposition was mingled with joy even in the very first Xmas so in our baptismal service a scene of persecution was enacted. An adopted girl of twenty—one who suffered much at the hands of her hysterical mother, had gained her consent to be baptized. But the mother, changing her mind, called the girl who had just received baptism, to come to the bank of the river. She then grabbed her by the hair and beat her unmercifully till we could rescue her and take her into our custody.

Among the fourteen baptized were six fine young people from two different villages where we have opened work and four from our own increased staff. This makes our whole group of Center workers professing Christians. On Xmas Eve from seven in the evening till after midnight we listened to the stories and confessions of faith or the fourteen to be baptized. They were so thrilling it made us forget the time as each told in detail of struggles and victory. One disillusioned ex-soldier told how he turned to Buddhism to find the answer to his problem but found it not, then to the study of communism, but found it not but did find what he was seeking in Jesus. A war widow, a young woman who had lost her husband by the atomic bomb in Hiroshima had returned with her baby to Kuji her former home. In here sorrow she had found peace in Jesus. Christianity was something new,

IV. After the War | 139

real and challenging to each and made some of us older ones feel very humble indeed. The meeting closed at one o'clock and then a few of our workers—but I was not among those present—arose before five and rejoiced the hearts and homes or many by their singing of Xmas carols.

One of our many Xmases was at one of the villages mentioned above—a place only about thirty miles from here but it took Mr. Yahaba and me just six hours to make the trip in two different buses, (you see why we long for a jeep) waiting for the bus to start and waiting at the exchange place etc. etc. This delay—the trip should be made in three hours—caused us to miss one of the meetings but we did get there for the evening Xmas service with about one hundred crowded into a small room. At the class we gave each an old Xmas card and one was heard to remark, "My, this has been a wonderful Xmas." Then a few of us sat up and talked till two o'clock and then we had to get up at five to get the six o'clock bus back to Kuji to prepare for another Xmas. We made good time returning and it took only three hours!

The kindergarten Xmas is always the first one and involves more work and joy than all the others I believe. One outstanding event on the program for "Grandmother Allen" was the English solo sung by my four year old Junko Yahaba. She was a bit appalled by all the people so her voice was not as loud and clear as usual. She was then worried for fear Santa had not been able to hear her and asked to try it again, for she did so want him to hear. She did and he did! Before the war the kindergarten had always given a little play, "Where Love is, God is" and this year we revived that and just before the beautiful pageant of shepherds and wise men offering gifts to the wee Mary and Joseph, little Martin the cobbler entertained guests while waiting for the visit of Jesus and then heard the voice, "Inasmuch as ye have done it unto the least of these ye have done it unto me". Preceding this, the orchestra performed with their new instruments and indeed made a "joyful noise unto the Lord". But Xmas would not be compete without the bags of candy from Santa (Portland Oregon and Lebanon Ind.) to say nothing of warm mittens lovingly kit by friends in Washington D.C.

Another beautiful Xmas was the candle service of our adult group of eighty, in charge of Mrs. Yahaba. Seventeen people from different villages around came to see this service and stayed in the Center for two or three nights. (Much extra works, but it was an opportunity to spread the Light). After this very impressive worship service we had a period of fun, playing kindergarten rhythms and games and orchestra. The Japanese have so little fun in their lives that it was a joy to see them really playing.

Then there was the S.S. Xmas and the Church service and finally the dinner for the staff—twenty-three—at my house. I had to take out all the movable furniture and have them sit on the floor around kindergarten tables—cramped and crowded, but we managed it. (However if the staff increases I cannot do it again.) The best part was the receiving of the lovely presents for each sent by my White Temple in Portland, Ore. I fear they eclipsed my good dinner.

Our last Christmas consisted of taking our gifts to the neediest families in Kuji and two nearby villages. All of our groups gave to the Christ Child and we took these offerings and gifts of L.A.R.A. clothing to thirty-five families. A truck company lent us a truck for a day as their gift and fourteen of us spent from nine thirty to four on Dec. 31st distributing the gifts.

The year 1948 marked the tenth anniversary of our Christian Center in Kuji, most of those years being very dark pre-war and war years when the Yahabas carried on in the face of persecution and all kinds of difficulties. So as we hear the bird singing these dark world days of December it is 'sweet to remember' that a great forward step has been taken and we are a bit nearer our great goal.

Thomasine Allen
Kuji, Iwate ken, Japan

P.S. IMPORTANT

We American missionaries have been granted A.P.O. which means that you can send straight to me by American mail. This will save you much postage and trouble in the sending of packages. I am going to ask however that you continue to send letters to me by Japanese mail at Kuji, Iwate Ken, Japan. My nearest American P.O. is three hours away and it will mean that I will have to have somebody there send things on to me. I am glad to manage someway about the packages for it not only saves you trouble and expense but will eliminate the opening of parcels in Yokohama but it will be more convenient for me if you send letters to Kuji. However if you forget and use the A.P.O. address it is quite all right.

[Report 11]

KUJI CHRISTIAN CENTER

1948-1949

It is the privilege of some to plant, others to water and tend the seed, but it is only God who gives the increase. The past year marked the completion of ten years of planting and carefully watching over the seed planted in Kuji, a place where the earth was most barren, watering it oft with "blood, sweat and tears". But God has been true to His promise and given the longed for increase.

=CHURCH=

The increase or harvest which has brought us the most joy and satisfaction was the two baptismal services—the very first in Kuji—and the organization of a church, the first church not only in Kuji but in the whole county of Ku no He, a county of twenty towns and villages and population of 100,000. On Sept. 26th the first baptismal service was held when fifteen were baptized and the second, on Christmas morning with fourteen receiving baptism in the little river almost in our backyard. On Christmas Day the church was organized and two important decisions made, one to sponsor evangelism work in a neighboring town and the other, to start a church building fund, hoping the day will not be too distant when a chapel can be built. We now meet in the library of the Center Building.

=SUNDAY SCHOOL=

The S.S. of about two hundred which we have carried on for ten years as a part of our Center program is now under the church and several of our new Christians have become teachers which necessitates a teacher training class. Two of the teachers at the request of the town authorities are starting Boy Scout work.

=CLINIC=

Russia is credited with the statement to just let Japan alone and she would soon destroy herself thru tuberculosis and venereal disease. This may be an exaggerated statement

IV. After the War | 143

but presents a very real problem. Because of the appalling health need in this town and district which in number one in almost every bad way, holding the highest infant mortality rate in all Japan, we opened a clinic last summer, using the sun porch of the kindergarten and the adjoining Japanese matted room. Until cold weather came to our doctor, Dr. Kinoshita, with three nurses served about one hundred people a day and this winter between forty and fifty a day, besides calls to far distant places. To release the Center rooms for their original purpose and to meet more adequately the clinic needs, we have received an appropriation and gift of money which will enable us to erect a small building this summer. Even though we have a resident physician, the Morioka Red Cross Hospital continues to send us specialists every two weeks for a general clinic and people come from far and near.

=KINDERGARTEN=

To me, the loveliest part of our work is the Kindergarten of eighty (120 now) tiny tots. We limit the number to eighty as we are trying to carry on a real religious educational program. We have had many American Occupation visitors and all have been most enthusiastic over the attitudes and skills developed here, and generous in their words of praise of our whole program and equipment. A group of mothers comes each day to make up the powdered milk furnished by L.A.R.A. and serve it to the children. The Prefecture of Iwate is asking us to take the children of those families on relief and say they will be responsible financially for them.

=W.C.T.U.=

Did you ever know of a W.C.T.U. to be made up of men and women and all young ones too! Well, that is what ours is, a fine group of seventy really working for peace, purity and prohibition. They have been so earnest in their crusade that they have organized branch societies in three other towns so that we really have a membership of about two hundred. A group of fifteen went to Morioka, the capital of Iwate recently to try to put some teeth in the enforcement of the purity laws. Thru public meetings, thru pictures, thru health education and personal interviews we are trying to make a dent in public opinion and practice along purity lines and the status of woman. Such a long uphill road, but the pilgrims are most enthusiastic and feel their responsibility to make Japan a better place. They are pilgrims with a purpose!

=BRANCH CENTER=

We have given birth to a branch center in Karumai, a town about forty miles from here but taking practically a whole day to get there. Two of our new Christians are from this village and are giving part of their house for meetings. Another room is being renovated and we will soon open a kindergarten. One of these Christians has been a school teacher for many years but she is resigning in order to devote her full time to the religious education of both children and adults.

=FARMERS' GOSPEL SCHOOL=

We have just completed our second Farmers' Gospel School with twelve fine young farmers selected from different parts of this county. Professors came from the State Agricultural Department in Morioka to give talks on various agricultural problems and these plus various members of our own staff formed the faculty. From the worship service at six in the morning till the end of the play hour at nine-thirty at night we tried to demonstrate Christian living and working together.

=OTHER WORK=

And what shall I say of the other forms of work—the work which takes so such time and thought and yet comes under no category.

Mr. and Mrs. Yahaba truly have the care of the whole flock, training and helping the staff of fifteen; keeping the doors of their hearts and homes open all hours of the day and night to those in need of material and spiritual help. Every day from early morning till long after midnight they are freely giving themselves to a constant stream of people. Their little four year old daughter, Junko, repeatedly saw her father drinking tea and talking to guests who had problems. So, seeing the former, but not understanding the latter, answered one day when asked what her father did, "Oh, he just drinks tea." Also they have taken into their large hearts and home a twelve year old waif whose parents were killed in the war and who was just riding the trains; and two eighteen year old boys just out of prison whom the Yahabas were asked to train.

Then there are the country trips which Mr. and Mrs. Yahaba and I take separately and together, speaking to large groups in faraway almost inaccessible places. We are trying to do something about these many, many villages and towns where there is no Christian work being done.

Our staff worship service at eight every morning starts the day with the one whom we are trying to serve as we endeavor to do our part in planting and watering the seed, praying that we may be indeed "wise workers" and "worthy worshippers" of Him who makes the seed burst into flower.

Thomasine Allen

[Report 12]

KUJI CHRISTMAS

1949

What a challenge, responsibility and pleasure it is to be able to bring to people for their very first time, the beautiful story of Christmas. Not only missionaries all over Japan, and Japanese pastors but the Occupation people by their generous gifts to worthy causes and their abundant good cheer are giving Japan something of the meaning of Christmas. In our far away isolated corner we too, joined the vast world family in celebrating the coming of the Prince of Peace bringing to many their first knowledge of Christmas.

On Dec. 11th we walked to a little village 2 1/2 miles from here where recently we had opened a S.S. in a private home. The wife had been one of our Clinic patients and she not only wanted to know more about Christianity herself, but wanted her children to have Christian training so one of the nurses and I go on Sunday afternoons—an hour's walking each way over bad roads and an hour for S.S. gets us back just before dark and in time for the evening service here. The flannel-graph story, Xmas songs and giving each an old Xmas card constituted their first Xmas and the 60 children and 10 adults crowded into the little room, sitting on the floor of course, were very happy.

Next was coming the Kindergarten Xmas on the 17th. Two of our men had gone to a neighboring hill and brought back a beautifully shaped Xmas tree so one evening was spent decorating that and making the manger from stacks of real hay. For always we close the program with the Holy

Night—wee Joseph and Mary over the Babe—Shepherds and Wise men bringing their gifts followed by the other kindergarten children and parents giving their gifts of money to the Child for the poor. My 'grandchild' Junko Yahaba sang in her clear little voice about the soft white blanket for the new born Babe. The orchestra performed with real gusto and "did themselves proud". Tolstoy's "Where Love is, God is", was given by a group of wee actors in a most impressive and effective way. Incidentally I had a Great Worry! For by the 14th only a part of the expected candy had arrived and what was I to do? The bags had not come either but I know we could make some out of colored paper—only it would take time—but what was there to put in them? The nearest army camp is a six hour round trip journey, but I got in touch with the authorities there and asked if, in case my candy did not arrive, could I beg, borrow, buy or steal some candies for the kindergarten and S.S. children. No American is going to let children down and especially at Xmas time so, do not worry about my morals, I did not have to resort to the last mentioned verb, and my mind was at ease. On the 15th a soldier made a long trip to bring me the candy and mountain of package and in one was a part of the expected candy and at least enough bags for the kindergarten though not the S.S. so rushed to improvise 200 at the last minute. (PLEASE, dear Santa Clauses, this next Xmas mail things in October, so I will not be subject to heart failure again.) The Chaplain has been most cooperative and helpful in getting mail to me and deserves a big vote of thanks.

The following day was the S.S. Xmas with the kindergarten repeating some of their program and the older

148 | BUILD UP, BUILD UP, PREPARE THE ROAD!

children giving "Why the Chimes Rang". As some beautiful dinner chimes had been sent to the kindergarten they were most effectively used at the last. Special attention was called to the children who had not missed a single Sunday and one little 14 year old was given a special ovation and a Bible as a gift. For she comes from a village many miles from here and has to leave here home about five o'clock in the morning, walk an hour to the train, ride in the unheated train for forty minutes, getting to Kuji at seven. She then plays around or reads in our Center library till S.S. begins at 9:30. As there are only four trains a day she has to wait till 3:30 in the afternoon (bringing lunch with he—ride back and then the hour's walk to her home—a whole day. But her father a Primary School Principal says it is her daughter's greatest pleasure to come here to S.S. She puts many of our Kuji children to shame.

The following day, the Chaplain of the Misawa Air Base and an officer drove over in a jeep truck—a drive of five hours over VERY bad roads. The truck was filled with toys women had collected and the men had 'restored' for our children, and a huge box of cookies they had made, which with a vast number of cupcakes I made, get us through several Xmases. This joyful, helpful serving on the part of various fellow Americans made a deep impression on the people here.

Thomasine Allen

[Report 13]

KUJI CHRISTIAN CENTER

The Year's Blessings   1949-1950

One of our missionaries once said, "We pray to God to bless our work and then when He does, we are greatly troubled. How very true! For budgets have a way of staying stationary more or less, while the work grows and needs multiply and one spends anxious hours on how to meet the increased opportunities.

Our Christian Center work has gone on a pace—the kindergarten of over one hundred; the S.S. of two hundred; the clinic averaging about fifty a day; the sewing classes three nights a week; the W.C.T.U. with its study and work groups; the country work in three surrounding villages—all a part of our little church. This church celebrated its first birthday by a baptismal service at Christmas time.

=BRANCH CENTER=

Karumai, a little town about forty miles from hare, in the mountains, has presented us with a real challenge. A school teacher who was seeking spiritual help, used to come in on the awful bus, frequently all during the war years to Mr. and Mrs. Yahaba who spent many, many hours talking with her. Thru this contact Mr. Yahaba, after the war was over started going out there once a month, holding a little meeting in this new Christian's brother's home. The brother and his wife followed the sister's steps and were baptized into our Kuji Church, along with several others from Karumai. These monthly meetings would generally begin at nine in the evening and last till midnight as some always wanted to talk after the formal meeting closed. Then the brother would talk with Mr. Yahaba till two o'clock or after. But these talks were very important. The brother said that he would give the adjoining house and lumber if we would repair it and open a branch of our Center. We did not realize when we accepted the responsibility that even so, it would cost us hundreds of dollars! Then we did realize it, we conferred with our pigs and told them to be fruitful and multiply as we needed the money that selling their offspring would bring. They responded beautifully—one litter having fifteen in it. Thru this and other ways we have managed to make a very lovely building out of an old decrepit house. The sister and another young woman have lived with us a year, working not only in the kindergarten to learn methods, but participating in all the Center activities so the Branch will be run in the same way as the parent Center. The dedication was in May and the day after, the kindergarten was opened with over sixty children. We have work in two other villages and are planning to do more, intensive aid extensive work when we have transportation.

=STATION WAGON=

Word came recently to us that friends in America that we should have a station wagon instead of just a jeep for which we were asking, as it could serve as an ambulance as well as taking us to the various villages where we have work and where we want to open new work. The burden of the twenty towns and villages of this county is on our hearts. The need of the station wagon which can serve as an ambulance was brought home to us recently when a man living about fifteen miles in the country put his wife in a push cart, then a bus, then a push cart again and finally got her to our clinic where our doctor was able to save her life but not that of the baby. Another man arrived early one morning with his wife in a truck. So the station wagon which is now definitely in sight will be one of the great blessings of the year. (It is due

the end of June.)
=NEW LAND=

In thinking ahead of the future development of the work, we needed more land but the owners of the land adjoining ours were not willing to part with it. Quite unexpectedly just as were wondering where to put the clinic building, they had a change of heart—and over an acre of land came in our hands. Now as soon as we can get sawmill which is unlawfully on the land, off, we can begin building our long waited-for and much needed clinic. Our doctor and nurses are carrying on in a remarkable way in cramped quarters and are succeeding in helping to lower the high rate of infant mortality—the highest in Japan. They are on constant call to the surrounding communities when clinic hours are over.
=MILK=

Thru the kindness of L.A.R.A. and the Baptist board as well as personal friends, we have been able to serve milk to our kindergarten children there times a week—and how they love it! Little fingers scrape the bottoms and sides of the bowl to get every bit. Needy babies throughout the community have also been given milk. For this and other nutritious foods, for White Cross boxes and the many boxes of clothing and supplies we wish to thank the generous American donors.

A recent investigation revealed that this part of the country called the Tibet of Japan, is at least sixty years behind Tokyo in every way. Well we could have told them that and saved them trouble; only I should have been tempted to say one hundred years. A Japanese educational report rates this prefecture of Iwate the very lowest in all Japan. All this makes our work many times more difficult and necessary and lonely. We are being urged to open a private Primary School for our kindergarten graduates so as to train up at least a few to have ambition for higher things.

The bad roads our station wagon will be called on to travel seems to be symbolic of the different road we are travelling I overcoming the ignorance and superstition so deeply entrenched in the minds of these country folk. But, like the station wagon we plan on getting over these roads—BOTH KINDS.

Thomasine Allen	or	Thomasine Allen
APO 7 Unit 3		Kuji, Iwate Ken, Japan
c/o Postmaster		
San Francisco, Calif.		

(Relief packages are not supposed to be sent by APO)

[Report 14]

WAGON WHEELS

Sept. 15, 1950
Kuji, Iwate Ken, Japan

August 17th was a real Red Letter Day, for the long looked for and anxiously awaited station wagon ordered last February arrived.

We received word the night before that the freight car with its precious burden had arrived in Kuji so in the morning right after our prayer service at 7:30, we all went to the station to tend to and to watch the unloading of our

IV. After the War | 153

welcome vehicle which had come from such a long, long way. We could scarcely wait to take off the many wrappings and see the lovely gray appear—and the red wheels. (We had our choice of gray or bronze and chose the former.) A large group soon gathered from nowhere and 'oh-ed and ah-ed' about it for they had never seen a car like that. It is the only station-wagon in all of Iwate Prefecture.

It so happened that Phyllis Beckley our youngest Baptist missionary, living in Yokohama was up here to see country work and also Mrs. Takegami one of the finest and most capable Christian leaders and speakers in all Japan was here to have some meetings. So they, with Mr. and Mrs. Yahaba, Junko, and I climbed in for the first ride, and the man who had come from Tokyo to deliver the car drove us home in style.

We drove it into the yard of the Center Building and all of the staff who ware here gathered around and we had a little service of praise and dedication. Mr. Yahaba read the passage in Matthew about going into all parts of the world with the Message, and each offered a prayer remembering in thankfulness the many donors from across the ocean, and expressing the feeling that they and we were clasping hands in a united effort to take the light into the very, very dark spot of Japan. And so it was dedicated to accomplish the work for which you sent it. I hope you can each feel a bit of our joy in having this beautiful means of carrying a beautiful message.

The Jeep seemed to understand Japanese though I will probably speak to it in English from time to time—for it started almost immediately to fulfill its purpose by going to a village about ten miles from here where Mrs. Takegami was to speak, and though next day it wont to Karumai, our Branch Center about forty miles away. It is so wonderful not to have to take the wood burning bus which is never quite sure whether it will get to the top of a hill or not. You will all receive our special thanks and blessings many, many times as we tour this district.

May the Wagon Wheels which you so generously sent, ever continue to turn to the many villages and towns and turn the people who are in great darkness to the Light. This will be the best thanks we can offer.

> Gratefully
> Mr. and Mrs. Yahaba
> Thomasine Allen

CHAPTER 3

"Training the Mind, Education"

[Note 2]

SOME THOUGHTS ON EDUCATION
Thomasine Allen

Education does not mean just knowing facts. Being able to apply the facts in daily living is equally important. An educated person is not necessarily one who has attended many years of school and made high grades as so many people believe and as is reflected in our companies and governments. The educated person must be able to draw generalizations and apply them to life's situations. To develop character and personality must be the highest aim, without which one cannot be called educated. Modern education has dealt largely with economics and industry, while the cultural aspects have been neglected. The humanistic achievements of mankind are the bases of real education.

In a democratic society the social heritage includes freedom of speech and religion; it also includes the arts, science, modern standards of living and economic opportunities for all. The social heritage is the things we believe in, work for, and have achieved. The door to this democracy is unlocked by education for all. Democracy is not only a political policy system; it is a way of life, respect for one's self and respect for others. Education gives everyone an equal chance. The school must teach this philosophy of equality and help directly to create such a democratic society, in addition to teaching the more factual matters. Education must give everyone the chance to improve his way of life and the way of life of others. It is this that we are striving for at our school.

It is said that Beethoven played badly when he performed in public for the last time—some notes were almost inaudible. WHY? The instrument was not sufficient for Beethoven's music. His musical education formal and personal, had taken him beyond the limitations of the instruments of his time. The sonata had been known for two hundred years enlarged and enriched it, lifting it into undreamed of power and loveliness. He was an emancipator. He took an old form of music and thru through study and application, improved it. He forced men to invent new instruments to match his art.

In the same way, our education must seek to develop people who are capable of challenging the limits and expanding the horizons of society, men who can create new solutions for old problems; men who make new music from old forms. We are like the instruments of Beethoven's time, net suited to the great potentials which surround us. Our

IV. After the War | 157

education must seek to provide not only answers, but healing and finer skills in the art of living which will bring to the world the benediction of power and beauty.

(1) Homare Educational Foundation (1952–2005)
Homare Elementary School (1952–95)

It was a little girl "Shigechan" who had moved from Hiroshima. She made Miss Allen hasten to establish an Elementary school. In the terrible scenes after the atomic bomb, Shigechan had walked looking for her father with her mother. Finally she found him alive but badly burned. She nursed him as best she could for the few days. Then mother and child came to Kuji, the mother's home. Shigechan attended Kuji kindergarten and spent a joyful time that helped to wipe out the memories of her wartime terrors. The compassionate allowance fed and clothed them, but man does not live by bread alone. Miss Allen worried, "what sort of schools are they going to prepare? What philosophy will they have? What goals are to be set? Could they teach "to believe and love each other? As one American what can I give the child who passed this terrible war time?" "God loves us, so we have to love each other".

Not only for Shigechan but also for all Japanese children, Miss Allen had great dreams to establish the elementary school.

158 | BUILD UP, BUILD UP, PREPARE THE ROAD!

[Report 15] memo

We knew that Christian Education limited to its general meaning of work in Sunday Schools and church was not enough when there were practically no Christian homes. So if we wanted the principles of Christianity to permeate the community we must not stop with the kindergarten but continue with Primary School and High School. This part of the work which we deem so necessary for the future going program is a real headache financially, to put it bluntly. The school is quite small for most people just do not understand. Only a few see the need and importance of character education—and we are thankful for those few. If we had this work in one of the large cities southward there would be no problem of enrollment, adequate tuition and parents who would be cooperative.

But here again we know that we are building a foundation or to change the figure of speech, we know that with "blood, sweat and tears", the desert is being watered and will someday "blossom at the rose", for the desert is not a place which God has forgotten.

Thomasine Allen
Kuji, Iwate Ken

The United States Education Mission to Japan, a committee of twenty-seven American educators, arrived in Japan. A report briefly noted that Iwate Ken stood at the bottom of the list in education. The northern area was at least sixty years behind Tokyo. Miss Allen commented "We could have told them that and saved them the trouble, only I would be tempted to say one hundred years." She emphasized that if the poverty-stricken northern area would not reform drastically and the community could not develop a friendly atmosphere, the educational condition would never change for a hundred years.

Once Miss Allen decided on a matter, she asked for donations from her many friends immediately. In 1952 the friends who lived in America rallied around Miss Allen and decided to help her works financially. Without their friendship and donations she could not have had a foundation and realized her ideal educational program in the Kuji area.

On June 20, 1952, Iwate Prefecture approved the plan of the Educational Foundation and Homare Elementary School. On July 7, as principal, Miss Allen opened the Homare Elementary school with five new pupils. "Starting a little primary school" meant a great deal more than merely welcoming five children into first grade.

> * Could we get children to come to the primary school? Would the parents see the advantages of a small private school? We knew that we couldn't charge very much tuition, and that the school would always be in the red, but it seemed to us that it might be the most effective way in which we could work and train leaders for the future, After much debate and much unwinding of red tape, we started a little primary school in 1952. (A. Hem., p. 136)

160 | BUILD UP, BUILD UP, PREPARE THE ROAD!

Although 125,000 students were enrolled in schools connected with the Christian Education Association in Japan, most of them were in high school and college; only a few thousand attended Christian primary schools. The Homare elementary school was one of the few Protestant Christian schools in Japan.

A member of the first graduating class, Mr. Toshio Fujimori who had retired as the principal of public schools, talked about Miss Allen and the Allen Junior College students with tearful eyes. He could not forget that she helped and nurtured him in all aspects. He wanted to be a teacher like her and intended to teach "you have to make much of one another—love each other."

(2) Seikei Dressmaking School (1953–63?)

Miss Allen said on tape, "I established a dressmaking school for young girls and women in this area. I was convinced that women had to get some technical skill for standing on their own feet and to be able to pass a happier home life."

On Feb. 17 1953, Iwate Prefecture approved the opening of the Seikei Dressmaking School. The curriculums were drawn not only in the art of dressmaking, but also, included "tea ceremony" and "flower arrangement" as Japanese manners. The class used to begin by reading the Bible and singing Hymns. An elderly woman said; "In our town, we could not find a sewing machine except at the high school. So, all of us were

IV. After the War | 161

excited to make dresses of our own sizes and designs."

Soon after Miss Allen took a trip to her home country, it was six years after the war. It was a journey to visit her supporters to express her appreciation for their help and to tell them about the development of the Kuji Center.

[Report 16]

THE BAGGAGE AND I

What a depth of moaning and drama-and work is in that one word "baggage"— loving hands that gave, loving hands that packed the forty-seven big trunks and boxes (two of which were pianos, one from White Temple, Portland, and one from the First Church, Seattle); friends who gave of themselves, time, money, thought, materials, and labor to make this ministry to hundreds and hundreds of folk here possible. The kindness and generosity of all on that side and the kindness of customs officials on this side who realized the purpose of my much baggage and passed it all thru quickly will not soon be forgotten.

Mr. and Mrs. Yahaba took the 22 hour trip down to meet, and were the first I could see as the ship slowly came in. Junk's delight was increased by the red zipper bag full of olives which was put into her hands immediately. Almost the last thing I did in Seattle was to jam another can of olives into the already full bag. Passengers on my nice freight boat had saved their oranges for her so she had here heart's desire and written request to me for olives and oranges answered.

The long, hand trip to Kuji was lightened by friends along the way coming to the train—some from a long distance. A stopover of two hours was made in Morioka, the capital of Iwate Prefecture, so as to call on the Governor and other State officials thanking them for past favors and bespeaking their good will in the future. (To get in and out of Japan politely is quite a chore!). Several stations from Kuji our 24 little children from out new Primary School got on the already crowded train to escort me to Kuji. There I had a real surprise for not only was the station packed and jammed, but it overflowed all around the building and the street was crowded with people to greet me, the Sunday School children, Kindergarten children, mothers, fathers—there must have been almost a thousand people. I finally waded and bowed thru to our station wagon. I felt that I had really arrived however when our staff and workmen—carpenters and painters (for much building was in progress) gathered on the Center playground for a thanksgiving prayer service immediately upon alighting from the car. The background of many apple trees in full bloom and a setting sun added to the beauty of this scene.

In another way I did not feel quite at home at first, for there were so many improvements and developments—now work, new additional workers and everything so lovely and beautiful, I told them that I had better take a furlough every other year. But when they saw the baggage I brought they decided I had better go every year. The dormitory building which houses many of our workers and also the little primary school we started last year was completed in my absence and is beautiful. Mrs. Yahaba would have made a wonderful architect or interior decorator or landscape gardener—but surely there is no place in greater need of her talent for creating beauty inside and out, than right here in Kuji. Near

IV. After the War | 163

the little clinic was an old house which they tore down and built anew adding more rooms for a beautiful, separate little hospital for tubercular patients. Then the foundation is in, and the lumbar purchased, and on the grounds to build a big annex to our present clinic building for we had to have more room to accommodate patients and take them out of the Center building where they are now. My first night back, one of our Japanese doctors brought back in the station wagon woman who soon gave birth to twin baby girls. A man bitten by a poisonous snake, and a little boy dangerously ill with pneumonia were also brought in and saved that night. This all made me keenly aware of the service our faithful staff was so unselfishly giving, morning, afternoon, and night. Many, many of you are having a real share in this, for every bit of money that was given to me during my furlough was sent out to Mr. and Mrs. Yahaba and that plus borrowing the equivalent of a few thousand dollars is making our increased hospital work possible.

There was a fooling of real humility and thankfulness when I compared the scene upon my arrival at the station and again at the Center as I looked at our beautiful grounds and buildings, with the scene on Dec. 8, 1941. Then, everyone on the street looked the other way and the one poor woman who did have the courage to bow was taken to the police office for questioning—why had she bowed to an American?? Yes, there were troubles and obstacles of all kinds which beset our beginnings and I too could say, "Thou hast set my feet in a large place" and "there are many adversaries", but when I think of the development of the last six years from a small kindergarten and S.S. in our Center building, with a very small staff to a staff of twenty-five, large kindergarten, a day nursery, fifteen S.S., a sewing school (afternoon and night meeting in the library), a primary school—the only Christian primary school north of Tokyo—a clinic and hospital, an organized church (also meeting in the library for Sunday morning and night services and various group meetings) and our Branch Center with its Sunday School and kindergarten in a town thirty miles away—the tribute of the hundreds of people at the station was to this work and a recognition of its worth to the community.

And so my baggage and I have arrived for my last term of service with the hopes that the various materials and supplies contained therein will make our work more fruitful and effective in bringing the Life Abundant to this needy section called the Tibet of Japan.

Thomasine Allen

Kuji, Iwate Ken, Japan

Mr. and Mrs. Yahaba and Junko join me in saying "Thank you to all."

[Report 17]

CHRISTMAS WHOLESALE

Dec. 26 in 1957

Those who have followed our Christmas during the last few years know that we have two heroes or heroines who play major roles in our many, many programs—a pig, grand tree in the Center and a little portable tree which goes from village to village in our station wagon carrying its decorations with it to be put on and taken off, put on and taken off, many,

IV. After the War 165

many times. Of course Mr. Yahaba and I 'also ran', while Mrs. Yahaba tended to all the thoughtful, detailed Christmas preparations for the Center program. The Big Tree was especially resplendent this year with new decorations.

Very early in December the phone rang, "Could you have Christmas in our school on Dec. 11th?" asked a Primary School Principal. Well, we did and from then on thru the 28th we had twenty-six Christmases! Eleven of them were in country schools, three in our Branch Center, six in Kuji Center and the others in village halls or private homes. Over 3000 thus heard the Christmas story and for many it was their first experience. The station wagon was as usual loaded with tree, cards, candy, pictures and decorations.

This year the winds, weather and roads seemed to be tempered to my advancing years. Of course it was cold and the program given in unheated rooms but it was bearable (wearing many layers of clothing) and the roads did not delay our progress as of last year and were really passable. As we bumped along in our faithful station wagon to the many country places, some of them forty miles away and some of them off the beaten track with no roads, the drabness of everything impressed me anew and I wondered how long it would be before the Light would shine transforming lives and surroundings. The beautiful autumn foliage which had given so much beauty and color to the scene was gone and the snow which conceals much of the ugliness and covers all with a mantle of purity, had not yet come, so there was nothing to relieve the drabness of the dirty, shoddy little shacks, called homes. This drabness of people and scenery was depressing and I wondered anew what possible joy these people who live and work in such conditions could have in life. Then as the road climbed to higher levels the distant scene, the beautiful mountains and vast expanse of sky reminded me that we must take the long view and not be too discouraged at the slowness of change. In time the drabness of home and life will be changed to color, light and joy as we endeavor to be creators with God of a better tomorrow.

To my greatly prejudiced eyes no Christmas could be any more beautiful and impressive than our various Kuji ones, the Kindergarten, the S.S. the Primary School, the Candle Service, and the Church worship service. My perfectionist co-worker, Mrs. Yahaba spares no time and labor to make the setting beautiful and worshipful. The Kindergarten Christmas which is always my favorite, was a little different this year as we incorporated in the Nativity pageant the story of When the Littlest Camel Knelt. Our 'littlest camel' vied in cuteness with the film strip of that story and when the grumbling little camel finally came under the influence of the Manager and Knelt in adoration it was indeed impressive and appealing.

From one village twelve miles away several of the young men have attended our annual Farmers' Gospel School and three are now waiting for baptism. One of them wanted us to have Christmas in his home. As they make their own charcoal they were rather lavish with it and to just see those bright red, glowing sticks made me feel warmer. First we had the children of the area, about 100, some walking for quite a distance, all crowded in a small space. All were eyes and ears for the bright Christmas tree and the picture stories. When they left at nine o'clock about forty adults remained for their meeting and believe it or not those people listened in rapt attention to Mr. Yahaba's talk of two hours! The father of the young man who invited us is quite a drinker but his son pled with him not to drink for one day at least out of courtesy to Christmas and us. The old man complied with the request and was the most eager listener of all, never taking his eyes off Mr. Yahaba as he told them how the coming of the Christ Child into his heart had changed his whole life. Human problems and suffering are the same and as the old man listened a change began to come over him and he later told his son, "If that is what Christianity is and does, I will withdraw my objection to your baptism." We arrived home at 1:30—in time to go to bed and start all over again the next day.

In most of the school Christmases we were asked to have meetings for the adults afterward so each place consumed many hours, but we felt more than repaid by the keen interest of young and old alike, manifested in the many questions during the discussion period.

On the 28th the little tree asked me, "Is Christmas all over for me now?" "No, you have one more appearance tonight." "And the little tree preened itself—surely if tonight is the last, it will be a large gathering and I will sparkle with my electric bulbs and decorations the very best I can." Our station wagon was loaded once more and then Mr. and Mrs. Yahaba, three of our young men teachers and I climbed in! Like the Littlest Camel our Littlest Tree was at first disappointed for it was taken to a small, dark house with one oil lamp, so its electric bulbs could not be used; the room was small and the audience was not keen eyed children but eight men in rough work clothes, four carpenters and our four farm staff. The little house with no electricity was on our 125 acre farm given us by this Prefecture to develop a Christian dairy farm and school. The barn and silo are completed and the carpenters are now starting on the agricultural school. It was so quiet and peaceful and as we sang carols by the little tree in the soft glow of the lamp, the first Christmas seemed very near indeed. Then we cooked our rice supper over the charcoal fires and washed dishes by flashlight.

And the little tree was happy with its very last Christmas, and even though it knew it could not be there for the next Christmas when the work and school would be in full swing, it felt honored that it could grace the first Christmas on our farm and add its beauty.

Thus ended our twenty-six Christmases (the little tree had been dressed and undressed over 20 times) with a hope, prayer and faith that our theme, "I am the Light of the World" will become a reality for these people sitting in darkness.

Thomasine Allen

Kuji, Iwate Ken, Japan

(3) Homare Middle School

The Homare Educational Foundation applied for establishment of Homare Junior middle school, and it was approved on January 29 1958, by Iwate Prefecture.

* Education in Japan has not been conducive to thinking. To quote from a recent Japanese magazine article," The Japanese, especially those who have traveled abroad, now often comment on the lack of emphasis on logic in Japanese business and education. The quickest way to paralyze a

classroom of Japanese students is to ask a question stressing reasoning." We are trying to overcome this is in our own small way. (A. Hem., p. 137)

Mr. Mitsuo Miyako ex-principal of this school, who was devoutly religious, wrote the education program of this school.

"Homare" means "the Glory of God". The aim of our school was all-round education; bring up intelligence and fine character. For the curriculum was separated into three courses; study by textbooks, study of living and study of social events. Some students lived in dormitories with several teachers.

(4) The Christian Dairy Farming School
(Feb., 1958–Feb., 1991)

"Of Many Men on Little Land"

There are the roads always narrow and mostly
        at the wood's edge or the river's.
There is the straw piled on brushwood bridges
        off the loan and the trees
only growing at the god's house, never in the
        fields.
There are the whole plains empty of roofs,
        squared into flats of water, no inch for
        walking but the dike backs, not so much
        as a green weed at the foot of the tele-
        graph poles or a corner patch gone wild.

> There are the men under moonlight in the
>   mountain villages breaking the winter
>   snowdrifts on the paddies to save days of
>   spring.
> There are the forest floors swept clean and the
>   sweepings bundles into careful, valuable.
> There are the houses without dogs, the farms
>   without grass-eating cattle....

> (Hem., p. 138, "Of many Men on Little Land,"
> *Fortune Magazine*, Sep., 1936)

Japan is mountainous and only about twenty percent can be cultivated, therefore the fields and paddies must be farmed intensively. The climate of the Kuji area was too severe to produce good crops. The season was short for double-cropping, and besides, the soil was very poor. After rent and taxes were paid to the landlord, the farmers were suffering from a food shortage.

Miss Allen intended to raise the standard of living and spread healthful diets in these farmers' villages in this area, so she had begun to work on the establishment of a Dairy Farming School and a farm. If the farmers lived in cozy homes with a steady income, it would not be surely difficult for them to understand the words "love of God" much less "Love thy neighbor." She wanted strongly to guide them to a joyful life and pleasant work. Real happy life was to come by not only in the riches but in the peace of mind in God.

IV. After the War | 171

In 1948, the Kuji Christian Center began the Farmer's Gospel School and twenty eight young peasants attended to learn something of improved farming techniques. They raised two pigs with garbage which they collected from several houses in the town. Soon they could finance by selling pigs.

When Miss Allen and the Center had the idea of starting a farm and a Dairy Farming Gospel School, they had no financial resources, but only a mounting enthusiasm for it. Again, she had been busy to write letters imploring for donations. It must be told that she gave all her savings kept for retirement in the U.S.

#1 Four Heifers and the Land

In 1955, two close friends visited Miss Allen from America, on their way to the Baptist World Alliance Meeting in London. When they heard about her plans, they called on their friend in Tokyo at once and made arrangements for four Jersey heifers to be sent to Kuji with the next shipment. Although the heifers were a gift, the consignee had to pay for the transportation. In 1955 and 1956, the four heifers were sent to Kuji. They had to go through complicated formalities to import the cattle. It was a big day when the cattle finally arrived at Kuji and were settled in stalls built next to the Center building.

172   BUILD UP, BUILD UP, PREPARE THE ROAD!

[Document 4]

JAPAN CHURCH WORLD SERVICE
in affiliation with
THE NATIONAL CHRISTIAN COUNCIL OF JAPAN

CHAIRMAN: REV. Y. MANABE
  TEL. 56-4774
   CABLE: OIKUMENE TOKYO   KYOBUNKAN BUILDING
DIRECTOR: REV. HALLAM SHORROCK 2. 4 CHOME, GINZA
ASSOCIATE DIRECTOR: CHUO-KU
 REV. KENTARO BUMA   TOKYO, JAPAN
TREASURER: MR. JOHN F. FAIRFIELD

> 540 Takakura Hino Machi
> Minamitama Gun,
> Tokyo To
> Dec. 13th, 1955

Miss Thomasine Allen
Kuji Christian Center
Kuji Machi, Iwate Ken

Dear Miss Allen:

Yesterday I went down to Yokohama to see the quarantine office again about the four cows they are still holding. I asked particularly about Jersey S71 and was told it would be released in another week or two probably. So please hold yourself in readiness to send someone down to accompany this Jersey to Kuji. We will probably have to notify you by telegram when the time comes.

Among the Jerseys you have already received there should be one with Ear Tattoo #1296 in place of #117 as I had previously informed you. This was an error on my part for which I am very sorry, but which must be corrected to keep the registration papers straight.

IV. After the War | 173

Will you please return the information sheet and ribbon for #117 which I sent to you and tell me just what you have done so far about the transfer of registration. I need this information right away.

If by any chance you do have Jersey #117 there and not #1296, then all is well and you can simply return the enclosed ribbon and information sheet for #1296.

One other matter I must bring to your attention concerns the distribution of female calves. It is important that as soon as the first calf is born to any of the heifers you have received you notify me and the secretary of the Iwate Ken Heifer Advisory Committee, Mr. Paul Gregory, in Morioka. We should know the date of birth, sex of the calf, and tattoo, and/or registration number of the mother.

Bull calves you are free to dispose of as you wish, but the first heifer calf of each cow is to be given away under the direction of the Iwate Prefectural Committee with the approval of our central committee. Of course you are free to make suggestions as to likely recipients. Such persons should apply to the Prefectural Committee using application forms which you can obtain from Paul Gregory.

[Document 5]
JAPAN CHURCH WORLD SERVICE
in affiliation with
THE NATIONAL CHRISTIAN COUNCIL OF JAPAN

CHAIRMAN: REV. Y. MANABE
      TEL. 56-4774
      CABLE: OIKUMENE TOKYO   KYOBUNKAN BUILDING
DIRECTOR: REV. HALLAM SHORROCK   2. 4 CHOME, GINZA
ASSOCIATE DIRECTOR: CHUO-KU
 REV. KENTARO BUMA   TOKYO, JAPAN
TREASURER: MR. JOHN F. FAIRFIELD

540 Takakura Hino Machi
Minamitama Gun,
Tokyo To
February 7, 1956

Miss Thomasine Allen
Kuji Rural Center
Iwate Prefecture

Dear Miss Allen

I am sending you herewith the information sheet and tag for the final Kuji heifer. I know you will contact the donor and keep him informed.

Since it is very important for registration transfers and also for our records to know exactly where each heifer is, I wish you would check the identification numbers on all the heifers you have received and send me the list of numbers. Apparently a number has been misread somewhere along the line.

In each case where the number on the animal corresponds with the identification number on the donor's sheet I sent you, will you please write directly to the donor asking for registration transfer papers if the heifer is registered. In case the heifer is not registered you might ask for any available information regarding its sire and dam.

When you have assembled these papers, take them to the Iwate Ken Norinsho (The Ministry of Agriculture) and inquire about registration procedure.

If you find that in any case the identification number on the animal does not correspond with that on the papers I've sent you please return the papers to me and tell me the true number of the heifer in question.

IV. After the War   175

I hope all is going well with the Kuji heifers and that you are keeping in touch with the Iwate Prefecture Heifer Committee through Rev. Paul Gregory concerning the distribution of female calves. I must have the date of birth, sex, and the number of the dam for each calf born, and would appreciate at least one copy of the best pictures you take.

Thank you so much for all you are doing for the Heifer Project

> Cordially yours,
> Alden E. Matthews, Secretary
> Japan Heifer Advisory Committee

AEM: mf
cc. Shorrock

[Document 6]

P. O. BOX 71
R Andolph 2-0086

Sunshine Farm Dairy
Jersey Milk and Cream
"The World's Finest"
MERCED, CALIFORNIA

January 29, 1957

Kuji Rural Center,
Kuji Kuji Cho Kuji Shi,
Japan.

Gentlemen:

Enclosed you will find the registration certificates on the cattle which we sent you last year, transferred to the Center.

We hope the cattle are doing well and will continue to

do well for you.

With best wishes, I am,

Sincerely yours

E. E. Greenough

[Document 7]

E. E. GREENOUGH

JAPAN CHURCH WORLD SERVICE

Kyobunkan Building

2. 4-chome, Ginza. Chuo-ku

Tokyo, Japan

Mr. Gerald Leach

16734 Ave., 17,

Madera, California.

Dear Mr. Leach:

Enclosed are a few pictures of the heifer you gave to Kuji Rural Center. These were taken last year, so things are much different now; but I thought you might be interested in them just the name.

Kuji Center is located in Iwate Prefecture, the most backward area of Japan. It is sometimes called the "Tibet" of Japan. Miss Allen, no doubt, has written and told you about the school, hospital and farm which they now have. The Center is making a real contribution to the community. I got a firsthand look at it during my visit there. Both Miss Allen and I wish you could visit the Center sometime.

I am enclosing a small article from a Japanese newspaper about the recent shipment sent to Hokkaido. There was a similar article, I am sure, on the heifers sent to Kuji. The heifers for Hokkaido were given to "pioneer farmers", a term

IV. After the War | 177

used for farmers who have accepted the governments offer to settle on poor, virgin land up in the mountains or in the cold areas of the country. Their crops are destroyed every three or four years because of the cold; so dairying is the only livelihood which can withstand the frequent disasters. I hope you find the Japanese writing interesting.

Are you studying Japan in your church this year? In any case, you have made a personal and significant contribution toward the welfare of the needy here. Thank you!

Please write if there is any way that I can be of service.

Sincerely,
Albert W. Huston

AWH: ma
cc: Miss Thomasine Allen

The government had land for a project to set up a demonstration farm in the Kuji area, but lack of a budget, heavy farm machinery, and most of all, experienced leadership had hindered its development.

The governor of Iwate Prefecture, Mr. Kenkichi Kokubun understood the conditions of the farmers in the northern area and had always been concerned over how to improve their standard of living. He was one of the good friends of Miss Allen and had a high respect for her Center work at Kuji. So he did all he could do for her proposal. After his death, his successor Mr. Senichi Abe continued the negotiations between the government and the Center.

He said, "If Miss Allen says" I will do it" then she will do

178 | BUILD UP, BUILD UP, PREPARE THE ROAD!

it. We can trust her." On January 1, 1957, the negotiations were finally completed, and the government leased 125 acres of the wild hill land to Miss Allen for use as a demonstration farm and an agricultural school. It was a very rare matter that the government leased national land to a missionary.

During the war, trees on the hills were cut down to make boats and left wild. Many refugees lived here to clear the land for cultivation.

The neighbor farmers were skeptical about this project, for they all knew that this wasteland never grew anything. They were sneering, "The chances would be slim."

Work was started at the farm at once, but clearing the land was making slow progress. Again, American friends helped Miss Allen by sending a big tractor and seeds of alfalfa; by and by the land was cultivated and became rich.

With government help and encouragement, a school building was constructed and a two-year course in vocational agriculture school was started.

[Report 18] =memo

Big need as we saw it was the barren life of the farmer, the forgotten man. How could we help to improve his lot? The Governor of the Prefecture knew our purpose and our desire and made available to us 125 acres of land on which they had wanted to have a demonstration farm but did not have the money or leadership to develop it. We sprang into action. Friends in America gave us a Ferguson tractor with several

IV. After the War | 179

attachments so we reclaimed part of the land, fertilized, planted and harvested. We erected a barn, and now have twenty-four heifers in it (four Jerseys came from America), and built an agricultural school.

Thomasine Allen

#2 Opening Ceremony of the Iwate Dairy School and Dairy Center

Celebration Party for Miss Allen Recipient of the Order of Sacred Treasure

In Feb. 5 1958, Iwate prefecture authorized to open Iwate Dairy School and Dairy Center. On July 3, the opening ceremony was held. In front of many guests, students and many farmers, the congratulatory speeches went on. Dr. Kagawa sent the words of praise and encouragement.

At the same time, Miss Allen received the Order of Sacred Treasure Gold and Silver Rays from Emperor. It might be a double pleasure for them.

[Document 8]

Greeting by Dr. Toyohiko Kagawa on 3 July 1958
Translated to English by Y. M.

I'd like to tell you my sincere congratulations on this opening school today. When we think about dairy in Japan, we found that it was run by predecessors in the early Meiji era who were influenced by Christianity and knew well the situation of advanced countries. They did not think about their own profits at that time. It is really the expression of Christianity to show the way to guide national nutrition, progressive way to solve the problem of provisions, a direction of new born

Japanese agriculture.

In Meiji era, Mr. Motozawa who started to run the dairy with the spirit of Christianity was expected to be the director of the political and economic world had the important role to formulate the basis of dairy in the history of Japanese dairy.

Dairy has the important role more and more for today's Japan. Further more, the dairyman has so much hardship in technical and economic aspects. By opening this school, today's dairy is expected to be progressing more and more, to be produced cheese and butter of course, and scientific research on all dairy products.

Especially, in the time of difficulty of the farm village which is losing spiritual backbone, I sincerely hope that practical farmers and directors who are trained well under the doctrine of Christianity of this school will be born. I'm really pleased with the opening school today, which involves suitable time and place. I praise for the holy name, and pray for the God's blessing and glory in prosperity.

[Report 19]
SEEDTIME AND HARVEST

1958

1957 has seen two major developments in the history of the Kuji Christian Center: the opening of our Junior High and the starting of our Dairy Farm.

=RELIGIOUS EDUCATION=
<Kindergarten>

Religious education with the emphasis on both of those

words is a 'must' in extending the Kingdom of God in Japan and especially in rural areas which are so backward in every respect.

The Center's educational program begins with two year-olds and continues to teen-agers or Junior High. The Kindergarten was our first project and thus our oldest avenue of service, for that was about all we could do before the war. During the war the Yahabas kept it up in spite of all sorts of difficulty and in spite of the destruction of the town of Kuji by fire. At that time the enrollment dropped to five. After the close of the war the number went up to one hundred and more. In post-war Japan kindergartens have become very popular and have sprung up like mushrooms, Christian ones, Buddhist ones, private ones end public ones. A Christian kindergarten in a non-Christian community cannot do much more than lay a few foundation stones in character building. It must be followed up by a Christian Primary School to be really effective.

<Primary School>

In 1952, mindful of the need of a continuing religious educational program we opened our Christian Primary School, giving it the name HOMARE, meaning 'praise'. We started in temporary quarters and each year since then we have juggled rooms and children to make places for all the grades. And we are still in the juggling act! Financially we could not afford this piece of educational work and it remains our biggest red ink item, but neither could we afford not to have it when we thought in terms of a Christian society and raising up future leaders, and not in terms of dollars and cents. Tuition is very small and the classes small and so the income is small. If we were in a city our Primary

School could be much more than self-supporting, but not in this rural area. When we opened the school we had to take the responsibility for all the years of compulsory education which means thru Junior High.

<Junior High School>

We opened this in April 1957 with our Primary School graduates and three others from neighboring villages. Financially it was a very hard step to take as the class is small and additional teachers and equipment necessary, but it had to be done so we did it. The little class has wonderful opportunities and we are hoping great things for them and expecting great things from them.

=MEDICAL WORK=

<Clinic and Hospital>

Our hospital reputation and sphere of usefulness have had been steadily growing. 1957 has brought some very fine additions to the staff and thus increased opportunities for service. A Christian hospital is different from ordinary Japanese hospitals in cleanliness and kind treatment. While we still cannot find a Christian doctor, our nurses are Christians, and in many, many ways let their light shine. One said, recently, "I am the most fortunate person in the world to be able to work here." Our station wagon still performs valiant service in carrying medical skill to far-away places, and from far-away places many patients come to the clinic.

=DAIRY FIRM CENTER=

This is probably our oldest dream come true. When we came to Kuji twenty years ago, one of our main reasons was that we might help these poor farmers whose lives are

IV. After the War | 183

so terribly drab in every way. How could we give them the abundant life with all that that means!

It was not much that we could do in the hard years just before the war. Then came the war, internment and my absence from Kuji of five years. But the Yahabas kept the dream in their hearts and it gradually began to take form, for during the lean war years they had to raise potatoes to keep from starving as there was no money to buy rationed food. Nearby farmers were surprised that our potatoes were so much better than theirs. To bring the dream into fuller realization we started raising and selling pigs. With this first money we opened our first Farmers' Gospel School ten years ago. This has been kept up every year. Interest grew in every phase but especially in cattle raising, for the Prefectural Government was anxious to change the diet or supplement it with milk and butter. It was a great day when we bought our first cow. Then many friends helped in getting Jerseys from America for us, and our herd grew but not our land. It was not easy to have pigs, chicken and cows next door, as it were, to the school and hospital. Then came the offer of 125 acres of land, a gift to us from Iwate Prefecture for a Christian dairy farm and agricultural school. They had watched our work and knew that we could do what they could not.

May of 1957 saw us moving some of our cows and three young men, graduates of the Hokkaido Christian Dairy College, out to our new land, on which there was a small building which we could use. Immediate farm work was made possible thru a gift of a Ferguson tractor and several attachments. Despite the delay in starting we raised almost enough food for our cows. A silo was erected and a big barn, so we have really started. We are now erecting which will house our workers, student farmers and school. We plan to have two courses, one for Junior High graduates and one for older farmers—all working as they study. The farm is near the village of Ono, ten miles from Kuji. Our motto is, Love of God, Love of Man and Love of Soil.

=OTHER WORK=

Various Sunday Schools, Sewing and Cooking Classes, Bible Classes

Church, with preaching places in three villages.

Karumai Branch Centere

The village of Ono where our farm is, is about half-way between Kuji and Karumai, our Branch Center is. A Christian family there is responsible for this work of kindergarten and two Sunday Schools, under the leadership of the Kuji Center.

Christian work in Japan is not easy, especially in rural areas where they are wedded to custom and tradition, but all the more needed.

It seems at discouraging times that the seed mostly falls in hardened places, in shallow ground and among the thorns, but SOME of it falls on good ground and it is from that, that we know in due time there will be a harvest of seed and souls, thirty fold? Sixty fold? One hundred fold?

Thomasine Allen

Kuji, Iwate prefecture, Japan.

IV. After the War | 185

[Poem 3]

LIVING IN JOYFUL EXPECTATION

Thomasine Allen

Praise the Lord!
Give thanks to the Lord, because He is good;
    His love is eternal.
Who can tell all the great things He has done?
    Who can praise Him enough?
I depend on God alone,
    For my expectation, is from Him.
    In Thee, O Lord, do I hope.
I will wait for the Lord
    And I will hope in Him.
I will wait in continuous expectation,
    I will praise Thee again, and yet again.
All the day long Thy saving acts
    Shall be upon my lips.
Truly my heart waits silently for God,
    My hope of deliverance comes from Him.
In truth, He is my Rock of deliverance,
    My tower of strength, so that I am unshaken.
Therefore my heart is glad and my soul rejoices,
    Moreover, my flesh will dwell in hope.
"The Lord is my portion," says my soul,
    "Therefore I will hope in Him."
I will hope in the Lord,
    This time forth and forever.

#3 The Deluge and Relief Activities

After the ceremony, immediately a big typhoon hit the town. From the South Pacific the storm swept across the islands of Japan, and destroyed a lot of towns. Kuji took the full violence of the storm. Its strong winds and its torrential rains left floods. Water rose in the river and the surrounding fields were flooded. Finally, Miss Allen became a victim herself, but all of people were safe and the house still stood.

Miss Allen told her friend;

> * I am now sitting in the midst of the debris, thinking of how many times during my long years in Iwate I have done relief work through famine, fire earthquake, and tidal wave; and now at the end I have become a victim myself. It is a good experience, even though I would not have chosen it.
>
> So, long with a backache, there was a real heartache, for where was the money to come from? As the damage to the buildings was assessed, I estimated that the repairs and replacement costs would total nearby $20,000. However, we were not unmindful of our blessings, especially when we thought of the many villages which were wiped out completely; we were safe and had roofs over our heads. We were getting the hospital ready first, for disease was breaking out, and we had to on the job. (A. Hem., p. 146–7)

At the very beginning, the Presbyterian chaplain came to help her from the US Air Base at Misawa. As soon as Miss Allen became relieved, her sense of humor returned.

IV. After the War   187

* I told the Presbyterian chaplain who came that, if the Baptists didn't help me out, I would join the Presbyterians, and that would be a terrible blow to both denominations! The heartache was also alleviated and worry lifted when the Baptist boards sent emergency financial help, and friends and churches who believed in Kuji rallied to raise money to repair the damaged buildings and replace the waterlogged supplies. It was a heart-warming experience to see the many, many friends the Kuji work had and the response they gave to our needs, it was like a beautiful rainbow after the flood. (A. Hem., p. 147)

[Report 20]

Christmas in 1958

One was a carpenter and he said he was going to remodel his house so that one room can be a real "meeting-house". Two of the three make charcoal in the winter when they cannot farm, (mountain-side farming at that). Incidentally a charcoal burner; one who cuts the trees, carries the wood to a big clay oven, and keeps the fire burning day and night, makes about eighty cents a day. The two said that they always carry a New Testament in their pocket and whenever a chance offers they read and sing hymns. The trouble with the latter, however, is that they cannot always remember the tunes. Well, about midnight they took off my decorations and we started home. But a real blizzard had come and the winding road was hard to see through the snow, so we had to inch our way along, arriving in Kuji about two o'clock in the morning. But nothing daunted we started out again at nine o'clock for another faraway place.

The last day, the 29th was perhaps the hardest day of all for on that day traveling through two and three feet of snow we had three Christmases and not one minute to eat our rice-ball lunch which we had brought with us. We were gone from nine in the morning to ten at night. Two of these Christmases were with groups of thirty and forty families who were repatriates and to them we took warm clothing in addition to candy, cards, etc. Going to the first place we knew we would have to walk for over a mile in the snow and that several would have to carry me and all the baggage on their backs, so what was our delight when we saw fifteen or twenty ragged children and two men with a long, low home-made sled drawn by a horse, awaiting our arrival at the turning off of the main road. They put me and the other baggage and Miss Allen on the sled, and away went the horse. That was a wonderful ride! Then in the little village office in a room about twelve by twelve they put me in a corner and decorated me, while about one hundred children crowded in and thirty adults stood in the entrance and at the "windows. After the program of songs, stories and pictures, the children received their candy and cards and left, while the adults waited to hear more from Mr. Yahaba and to receive the clothing which we had brought. Then much to my surprise, each family presented us with a bag of beans; red beans, white beans; all kinds of beans. They have so little themselves it hurt us to accept but it would have hurt them more if we had not accepted. So we were glad to have the horse and sled return us and our beans to the waiting jeep at the main road.

From there at about two o'clock we went to another repatriate village, near our farm. In the upstairs of this new

IV. After the War | 189

village office, about one hundred children and parents were waiting for us and had been there since morning. It was their first Christmas.

At about six pm, we arrived at our dairy farm where they decorated me for the last time. I was glad to shed my final beauty in a place that holds so much promise for the future.

Thus end the stories of the 1958 Christmas by the two trees. In conclusion they said, "Two things especially have pleased us; the fact that so many adults expressed a desire to have a New Testament, and that all of the country places urged Mr. Yahaba to return in February during the holidays of the old New Year and talk a LONG time, (evidently two hours were not enough!)

The Trees join me in thanking friends far and near, in Japan and in America for making these many Xmases possible. The theme for the Center programs was, "I am the Way." Will you please continue your interest, help and prayers that as we go among the country folk, we may be able to guide their feet along the true Way.

Thomasine Allen

CHAPTER 4

*Retirement From Missionary Work
and Honorary Award*

On 1955, at the age of sixty-five, Miss Allen retired as missionary of the American Baptist Foreign Mission Society (ABFMS) whose offices were located at Valley Forge Pennsylvania U.S.A. She could get certification to continue missionary work in Japan. ABFMS assumed full responsibility for the character and financial support of Miss Allen, including her return passage to the United State.

The Japan Fellowship of American Baptist Missionaries (JFABM) sent a paper and guaranteed her four matters;

1. Logistic Support in Japan.
2. Transportation for return to the United States.
3. That she will able by all rules and regulations of the Japanese Government.
4. Any other information will be gladly given.

After forty-one years in Japan, she found herself a

much-honored senior missionary. Her Japanese and American friends evaluated her ability and achievements, so she officially received several kinds of prizes.

(1) Iwate Prefectural Cultural Prize

On January 3, 1950, she received *an Iwate Prefectural Cultural Prize* from Iwate Nipposha (newspaper company), for her social work for education and community development of Iwate prefecture.

(2) Invitation from the University of Chicago

In 1950, her alma mater invited her as *a professor of the science of religion*. Her professor had nominated her to take over his position in his last will, and the faculty recognized it officially. This proposal touched her, but she would not change her mind once she had decided. "I could not go back on my words to God; I would stay Japan." She said that she had a hard time praying for a long time.

(3) The Fifth Order of the Sacred Treasure

On July 4, 1958, the Emperor honored her with an Imperial Decoration, *the Fifth Order of the Sacred Treasure*, for her forty three years working for social development in the rural areas. She was thanked by the Emperor and Empress on the palace grounds.

(4) The Testimonial of her Work on Social Welfare

On December 4, 1958, she was awarded from the National Social and Welfare Ministry by the Minister of Welfare; Ryugo Hashimoto.

(5) The Honorary Degree, Doctor of Humane Letters (L.H.D.)

The College would like to confer on her, *an Honorary Degree of Doctor of Humane Letters in absentia*. In April, 1959 she received a letter from President Harold W. Richardson, to invite her at the Commencement cerebrated for the 125th anniversary of the founding of Franklin College on June 7, 1959.

Later in 1960, at the March 2 Convocation, Miss Allen visited Franklin College and received a hood and robe for her honorary degree from President Harold W. Richardson.

> * It was a family affair; only those connected with the Center were invited, and it was held out of doors. The kindergarten performed nobly, each class by itself and then all of them together, and the Elementary school Middle school sang beautifully. There were speeches, and flowers were presented by smallest children. Afterwards they set up tables with all sorts of Japanese food, and we all had lunch together and special time, and then they sang some more songs. It was all quite lovely, and the Mothers' Club took the whole responsibility. (A. Hem., p. 151)

[Document 9]

The sentences of recommendation
Franklin College of Indiana
Franklin, Indiana

IV. After the War | 193

OFFICE OF THE PRESIDENT
THOMASINE ALLEN

Mr. President: Since very early days, sons and daughters have had equal place in the family of Franklin College. Accordingly, I have the honor to present the name of one whose fore bearers helped to found the College 125 years ago. The faculty has recommended that at the beginning of this anniversary year, the College honor Miss Thomasine Allen, class of 1911.

Miss Allen taught at Albemarle, North Carolina 1912, and then did settlement work in New York City. She became a missionary for the Women's American Baptist Foreign Mission Society in 1915, and sailed for Japan. Here she worked as a teacher and evangelistic missionary in Tokyo, Sendai, Morioka, and Kuji, her present location. She has experienced earthquakes, famine, and war both in large cities and remote back country areas. On December 8, 1941 she was interned and repatriated on the *Gripsholm*, December, 1943. She was in four different internment camps.

In 1945 she was a staff member of the Tule Lake Relocation Center in California for Japanese. In 1946 when the Center closed she returned to Japan.

Her work at Kuji, a rural Christian Center, was ministry to all sorts of needs and all sorts of people. She operated a county day nursery, school, hospital, and farm.

During the past 20 years the Center at Kuji has grown to five acres with ten buildings including a hospital, tuberculosis hospital, a clinic, workers dormitory, a church membership but no separate church building, three Japanese doctors,

194 | BUILD UP, BUILD UP, PREPARE THE ROAD!

four nurses, and a total of thirty workers. The work includes a day nursery, sewing school, and 15 Sunday schools in the county. This work has been enrolling many Japanese.

On July 4, 1958, Miss Allen was presented the fifth Order of Merit of the Sacred Jewel by his majesty, the Emperor of Japan, for her work among the Japanese people.

On September 30, 1958, a typhoon struck the center and the water caused considerable damage. The loss was estimated at over $5,000 and alumni and friends rallied to Miss Allen's plea for funds through Mrs. Carl Winters.

Miss Allen was retired in 1958, but has built herself a house at Kuji where she will spend her remaining years doing the work she loves; supervising a new agricultural project that has been her dream for years.

Mr. President: May I present the name of one whose entire career beautifully symbolizes the motto of Franklin College, "Christianity and Culture," who has combined learning with compassion in an area of great need, who has bridged the gulfs of race, nation, language, and cultural heritage, for the honorary degree, Doctor of Humane Letters (in absentia), Miss Thomasine Allen.

[Document 10]

The sentences of recommendation
Franklin College of Indiana
Franklin, Indiana

OFFICE OF THE PRESIDENT

APRIL 20, 1959

Miss Thomasine Allen
Kuji Iwate Ken Japan

IV. After the War | 195

My dear Thomasine:

In looking forward to the Commencement which begins our celebration of the 125th anniversary of Franklin College (founded in 1834) the faculty and Board of Directors would like to include recognition of the immeasurable contribution made by many Franklin alumni in the service of the Kingdom of God, in the farthest fields as well as here at home. Accordingly, because all of these folks, and all of us here on campus who know you, realize what a wonderfully helpful life you have lived in a remote part of Japan, the College would like to confer upon you at this Commencement, June 7, 1959, its honorary degree, Doctor of Humane Letters (L.H.D.). In your case, I know that circumstances will, in all probability, prevent your being here to receive it. Almost never does a college grant an honorary degree in absentia, but in your case there is absolutely no hesitation whatever.

If you find it convenient, it would be very good to have a brief message from you, not so much in response to the degree, as to the continuing challenge to Franklin College to send a goodly number of its people into the special services of Christ through his church. This need be only the briefest kind of message, so that it might be read at the Commencement program.

The love and good wishes of the entire Franklin family come to you with this message.

> Most sincerely,
> Harold W. Richardson

Dictated by HWR
Signed in his absence by jwh

[Document 11]
Franklin College of Indiana
Franklin, Indiana

OFFICE OF THE PRESIDENT

July 8, 1959

Miss Thomasine Allen
Kuji Iwate Ken, Japan

My dear Miss Allen:

I am enclosing herewith a copy of the citation read on June 7 as your name was presented for the honorary degree, Doctor of Humane Letters. The hood appropriate to the degree and the diploma are one their way in a separate package. To the best of my knowledge, this is the first and only time Franklin College has awarded an honorary degree in absentia. I do hope all the materials reach you safely.

May I add that this award gave us at Franklin a very deep satisfaction and the appropriateness of it, especially in the light of the purposes of the college, was instantly recognized by the audience and shown in its loud acclamation.

We shall continue to cherish the remembrance of your past visits to us and of your selfless labor among those you love. All good wishes to you in the months ahead.

Most sincerely yours,

Harold W. Richardson
President

(6) Honorary Citizen of Kuji City

On Nov. 3, 1959, Kuji City Council voted to make Miss Allen *an Honorary Citizen of Kuji* unanimously and gave her a silver medal.

By her enthusiasm, Mayor of Kuji; Mr. Gyobun Yamauchi and Mayor of Franklin; Mr. Frank S Records made a proclamation to be sister cities. Her real purpose was that the understanding of Center and the importance of spiritual training would deepen in Kuji. In 1960 when Miss Allen visited to Franklin, she delivered a greeting letter of the Mayor of Kuji to Mayor of Franklin in a ceremony at the City Hall as follows:

[Document 12]
> Kuji Mayor's congratulatory Speech
> translated by Y. MEGURO.

> From your city in 1915 came a young lady to work with us. She has had honors bestowed on her from your side of the Pacific and from our side.... In Japan as well as in America. Because we respect and honor Miss Allen and want her to spend her life here, we as a City Council in October, 1959 voted unanimously to make her an honorary citizen of Kuji.... Miss Allen has been a real bridge across the diving ocean and it is an honor for us to have her in our midst.

Even now, the two cities are actively maintaining friendly relations. Franklin College regularly dispatches English teachers to Kuji public high schools, and sometimes Kuji public junior high school students visit Franklin. In 2010, as one of the memorial events of the 120th anniversary of Miss Allen, the citizens of Kuji visited Franklin.

(7) Centennial Celebration of Protestant Missionary Activities in Japan

On Dec. 18, 1959, the Japanese Protestant Church had celebrated its centennial year in Tokyo. At that time, church members numbered more than 350,000. It was said, "Protestant Japanese professed a biblical and orthodox Christianity which emphasized doctrinal authority and exemplary moral behavior." Miss Allen had gone to Tokyo for the Centennial.

> * It was truly inspiring to see at least 10,000 Christians in one worship service; imagine that in Japan! Nearly all of the church congregations are so small that it helped all of us to be in a really big meeting. Like Jacob, I guess we all needed to see the wagons at times. Representatives from all over the world brought or sent greetings, and that made it worldwide in scope.
>
> In is hard to quate all of that with Kuji. For Tokyo and its churches belong to the twentieth century, and here in Kuji we are back where the first missionaries were in the nineteenth century. It is discouraging, but it is necessary, and maybe in another hundred years some results will be seen here, too. Do you remember the story of the man who had tried so hard to win people and was so discouraged at the small number? He talked it over with Jesus and came away smiling. When his friends asked him what made him

IV. After the War 199

so happy, he answered, 'Why Jesus said,' Four is a very large number indeed.' "Kuji has always had a large number! " (A. Hem. p. 152)

V

"The Way to Better Tomorrow"

Who are these that fly along like clouds,
Like doves to nests?

(Isaiah 60:8)

The APL liner the S.S. *President Cleveland* invited Mrs. McKenzie with Miss Allen in celebration of her 50th trans-Pacific ship crossing. After the celebration, on Jan. 9, 1960 they returned to the U.S. from Yokohama. Mrs. McKenzie was the first honorary citizen of Shizuoka City. In 1918, she first crossed the Pacific to Japan with her late husband, Mr. Duncan Joseph McKenzie, who had worked as a pioneer of a tea importing business in Japan. After he died, she still spent most of the year at her home and worked for Japanese child welfare in Shizuoka, and greatly helped Miss Allen. Both of the ladies had lived in Japan for more than forty years, and were honorary citizens of each town, so many newspapers, including the Japan Times, reported on their voyage. On Jan. 21, the ship arrived at San Francisco.

In March, Miss Allen visited and spoke at the Franklin College convocation. At the same time she was a guest of honor at a tea given by her sorority, Pi Beta Phi. Faculty, staff members and their families had been invited to meet Dr. Allen. At the Franklin First Baptist Church in the morning service, she also spoke of her experience with her love to God and Japanese people as a visiting missionary. One of the active missionary circles of the church was named in her honor.

CHAPTER I

Relief Activity

In 1960, the relationship between the United states and Japan was thrown into confusion. Several years earlier, a revision of the U.S.—Japan Security Treaty had proceeded. In January, American President D. D. Eisenhower and Prime Minister S. Kishi reached a consensus on the new bill. The Japanese government was planning to hold the signing ceremony in Tokyo on June 19, with President Eisenhower in attendance.

Many Japanese people strongly opposed to the revision of the Treaty, thought it might annul the Japanese Peace Constitution which vowed renunciation of war and demilitarization. The movement of the people grew stronger day by day, so that the President could not visit Japan and the Bill was approved naturally to become law. Miss Allen never commented on that issue.

On May 24, an enormous tidal wave from an earthquake that occurred in Chile, came to the northern coast line completely washing out several villages. Many lives were

204 | BUILD UP, BUILD UP, PREPARE THE ROAD!

lost and much damage was done, so she began another relief
trip walking from village to village sending her sympathy to
the victims. Again she wrote many letters to her friends and
supporters.

[Report 21]

AFTER THE TIDAL WAVE

1960

So much of life in Japan seems to be doing relief work—
earthquakes, winds and fires; floods, typhoons, tidal waves
and famines have been our lot and we who have escaped
have tried to do our bit in helping the victims. From the 1923
earthquake to the last tidal wave this year, nearly every year
has seen some catastrophe and many of these major ones
have been in this northern section.

The northern famine in 1931 took me on my first big
relief trip, walking over mountains and mountains along
the sea coast for 50 miles—an almost completely isolated
district. Then in two years the 1933 tidal wave which wiped
out villages and did untold damage, sent me on almost the
same course, leaving an unforgettable memory of death and
destruction. Then the 1960 tidal wave came from an earthquake in Chile (the world is one, for better or worse!) and
again the same territory was affected and afflicted, and sent
me on my third trip to the mountainous seacoast. But this
trip was quite different, Time Marches On, and makes roads
to march on, so instead of painfully climbing mountain,
there was now a brand new road winding around up and

V. "The Way to Better Tomorrow" | 205

over and thru the mountains. The scenery was breath-taking
in its beauty (if Mr. Hilton ever catches up with all this loveliness he will build hotels all over the place) and the road was
breath-taking in its danger. The road—narrow and nothing
but sharp turns and curves with the sea far, far below and the
mountain top far, far above—then a big truck bears down on
you from no place and you wonder how you are ever going
to pass each other—but eventually you do. At moments like
those I thought longingly of the mountain path I walked 29
years ago.

While travel was different and belonged to the modern
age, the tidal wave, destruction, the ability of people to pick
themselves up and press ahead, and the gratitude and friend-
liness of the people were the same. The newspapers and radio
knew of our trip and broadcasted it in detail, this brought
out many friends in different places and much picture-taking
which slowed us down. In one place a prominent man of
the community had been in my Bible class when he was a
H.S. student in Morioka. He brought his English hymnal
and wanted me to sing one of the songs with him.

Our caravan consisted of two loaded station wagons
and a big trailer all packed tightly with clothing, school
supplies and food. Money had come to me thru friends and
also many boxes of clothing—St. Margaret School in Tokyo
had sent 30 boxes—so we wanted to be good stewards and
give where the need was greatest— if there is a gradation of
need in nothingness!. The easy procedure would have been
to give all to various town officials but we wanted to make
it more meaningful, so before leaving divided the clothing

into categories—men, women, children and what age and grade in school, pre-school children and babies. Then we would get a list of the families having the hardest time and would make up a large bundle of clothing for each member of the family, school supplies for his or her grade, milk for the babies, packages of sweetened crackers, and the Gospel of John done in a very attractive booklet form. We stopped for this distribution in 17 places, ministering to over 500 people. In one place where a whole area had been washed away, the survivors had gathered little piles of lumber from the wreckage of what had been their houses, To be chosen as one in of a number to be honored by the Association for Japan-U.S. Amity and Trade Centennial, was indeed an honor, tho undeserving, and a tribute greatly prized, and humbly received.

There are many bridges between nations, bridges of diplomacy, politics, culture, trade, economics and religion. But it seems to me that the bridge of Christianity is the strongest of all, for spiritual bridges remain even though the others may falter and fail in time of stress and storm. It is because I believe this force to be the greatest in the world that I have dedicated my life to sharing these values with others.

After I had lived and worked in Japan for about twenty years, I decided that the greatest contribution I could make to Japan would be to go to some place, neglected and untouched and thus help one of the weak links in the chain which would in turn strengthen the whole. The church had become largely urban, dealing mostly with the intellectual

V. *"The Way to Better Tomorrow"*
207

and middle class and neglecting utterly many of the rural areas. After living and working both in cities and country I can understand better why this has happened. The same money and effort put into urban projects would bring forth visible results while work with people in backward, isolated areas, people of not much education, self-centered and satisfied with their narrow outlook and ways of doing things, does not produce much in the way of results you can see. One just has to have faith that a foundation is being laid for a noble structure others will build. Without this faith life would indeed be dark for the problems and discouragements are just too many!

Two Japanese co-workers and I made a survey and found one of the weakest links in the Japanese chain, in the northern part of Iwate Prefecture which is in the northern part of the main island. People in this large isolated area had lived their lives almost untouched by new ideas of any kind. Of course Christianity was unknown. So twenty years ago we came to Kuji which is the county-seat, to work in many towns and villages in the area. It has been and is a real rural pioneer work. After many weeks we were able to acquire about an acre of land at the edge of Kuji. Then after more trouble of getting carpenters, nails, and materials, we finally erected a very beautiful Christian Center Building, in 1938, and our first organized work was a kindergarten and Sunday school. Then the war came and blackness covered the land. I was interned but the work went right on. I was not to know till later all the trials and hardships our little group had, but their courage and faith never faltered.

At the end of the war when people were suffering so from malnutrition, we opened a free clinic with doctors coming from the Red Cross Hospital in Morioka, every two weeks. This eventually led to resident doctors and a hospital. At that time the infant mortality rate here was the highest in Japan so we helped to tackle that problem first and we are glad to know that we have had a small share in lowering the rate.

In all of our work and life here we have tried to see the need and meet it as far as possible. This has led to a varied program different from most mission work, and placed it in the center of their land. Those little piles of lumber told a sad story of suffering and loss and yet of courage to build and start all over again.

Thomasine Allen.
Kuji, Iwate-Ken, Japan,

CHAPTER 2

"I Have a Great Treasure that I Want to Share."

(1) The Association for
Japan-U.S. Amity and Trade Centennial

In 1860, the first Japanese Ambassador visited the United States. In 1960, the Japanese Government organized the Association for Japan-US Amity Trade Centennial, and held a centennial ceremony on November 10 in Tokyo. The association selected 300 American persons who had made contributions to Japan in religious and educational, economic and industrial, political and diplomatic, social and cultural fields over the 100 years.

Although the anti-Anpo demonstrations forced the Japanese government to cancel an invitation to President D. D. Eisenhower, they could not destroy the friendship built between the two countries through service and sacrifice, education and appreciation. (Anpo = security treaty between the

U.S. and Japan)

Miss Allen was invited to a big Citation Ceremony, chosen for a group for "social and cultural works".

> * The program was very lovely and dignified; we each had to go up and receive our citation, and there were several speeches and congratulatory messages by Mr. Kosaka, Minister of Foreign Affairs and by the American Ambassador.
>
> We were also given a large Urushi etching produce (a special type of lacquer print) of Japanese vessel, the *Kanrin Maru*, which took the first Japanese delegation to America in 1860. Then they had a truly remarkable film, The Bridge That Spans the Pacific, which showed the history of Japanese-America relations. Woodcuts were used to show life in feudal Japan, while photographs and newsreel clips were used for the later years. It was especially well done!
>
> In one part of the hall, pictures of many of the 298 people being honored were on display. There were pictured of many who had died or were retired in America, and it was good to "see" of my old friends in that way. There were seven Baptists on the list, and I am the only one still in Japan. (A. Hem., p.154)

When the reception was over, Miss Allen caught the train at Ueno station and returned to Kuji. It was nearly midnight when she could settle in her seat at ease, and think to herself. The train would carry her north through Sendai, Morioka and finally to Shiriuchi, to transfer to a local line.

V. *"The Way to Better Tomorrow"* 211

* Again I was reminded of the past: the long, cold treks over mountain, hill, and plain on relief trips during famine, earthquake, and tidal wave; the starting of day nurseries and kindergartens; beginning of medical and educational work for country folk. I was the "victim" of all these honors, but the real thanks and homage belong to Mr. and Mrs. Yahaba who, by their consecrated and dedicated lives, have made the Kuji work possible, and to all those who, by their prayers and gifts, have pulled me through the valleys and up the mountains. Perhaps I have learned through them a bit more about the necessity of lifting my eyes to the mountains when walking in the valley and keeping my faith that there is always *a high road*. Forty years had passed, and I retired from active service as a representative of the society, but not from Kuji. I was needed in the school, kindergarten, church, and so on. I was needed to help to carry the financial load. "I must live to get this place self-supporting—or anyway, so I think! It was not illusions now about what "this generation" could accomplish; instead I had an absolute faith in what God could do and had done. (A. Hem., p. 154)

In the morning the train had come to Morioka station. Vendors came to the train windows to sell passengers ice cream, box lunches and pots of hot tea. Seeing the grandeur of Mt. Iwate, Miss Allen remembered her first work in Morioka, 28 years earlier.

* It seems to me, as I look over the years, that God's message to me was, "I want to work through you in that isolated,

difficult place, and I will show you the way to soften the
soil. It must be by *blood, sweat, and tears*; the blood of sacrifice, the sweat of physical and spiritual labor, and the tear
of heartbreak, discouragement, and disappointment." Then I
thought of St. Theresa when she prayed, "God, if you treat all
of our friends as you do me, it is no wonder that you have so
few." (A. Hem., p. 156)

Again the train pulled into Shiriuchi station, where she got
off the train to transfer to a local line for Kuji. As soon as she
entered the waiting room, the stationmaster invited her to his
office, and served her hot tea and a bowl of hot noodles. The
train from Shiriuchi to Kuji was so small on a single set of
tracks that it took more than two hours.

  * As we bumped along the tracks, the drabness of everything
  impressed me again, and I wondered how long it would be
  before the Light would shine, transforming lives and their
  surroundings. The autumn foliage which had given so much
  beauty and color to the scene was gone, and the snow which
  conceals so much of the ugliness and covers everything with
  a mantle of purity had not yet come; so there was nothing
  to relieve the drabness of people and scenery was depressing,
  and I wondered what possible joy the people who live and
  work in such conditions could have from life. Then, as the
  train climbed to higher levels, the distant scene, the beautiful
  mountains, and the vast expanse of sky reminded me that
  we must take the long view and never be too discouraged at
  the slow pace of change. In time, the drabness of home and
  life will be changed to color, light, and joy as we with God

endeavor to be creators of a better tomorrow. (A. Hem., p. 157)

[Report 22] memo

To be chosen as one in of a number to be honored by the Association for Japan-U.S. Amity and Trade Centennial, was indeed an honor, the undeserving, and a tribute greatly prized, and humbly received.

There are many bridges between nations, bridges of diplomacy, politics, culture, trade, economics and religion. But it seems to me that the bridge of Christianity is the strongest of all, for spiritual bridges remain even the others may falter and fail in time of stress and storm. It is because I believe this force to be the greatest in the world that I have dedicated my life to sharing these values with others.

After I had lived and worked in Japan for about twenty years, I decided that the greatest contribution I could make to Japan would be to go to some place, neglected and untouched and thus help one of the weak links in the chain which would in turn strengthen the whole. The church had become largely urban, dealing mostly with the intellectual and middle class and neglecting utterly many of the rural areas. After living and working both in cities and country I can understand better why this has happened. The same money and effort put into urban projects would bring forth visible results while work with people in backward, isolated areas, people of not much education, self-centered and satisfied with their narrow outlook and ways of doing things, does not produce much in the way of results you can see. One just has to have faith that a foundation is being laid for a noble structure others will build. Without this faith life would indeed be dark for the problems and discouragements are just too many!

Two Japanese co-workers and I made a survey and found one of the weakest links in the Japanese chain, in the northern part of Iwate Prefecture which is in the northern part of the main island. People in this large isolated area had lived their lives almost untouched by new ideas of any kind. Of course Christianity was unknown. So twenty years ago we came to Kuji which is the county-seat, to work in many towns and villages in the area. It has been and is a real rural pioneer work. After many weeks we were able to acquire about an acre of land at the edge of Kuji. Then after more trouble of getting carpenters, nails, and materials, we finally erected a very beautiful Christian Center Building, in 1938, and our first organized work was a kindergarten and Sunday school. Then the war came and blackness covered the land. I was interned but the work went right on. I was not to know till later all the trials and hardships our little group had, but their courage and faith never faltered.

At the end of the war when people were suffering so from malnutrition, we opened a free clinic with doctors coming from the Red Cross Hospital in Morioka, every two weeks. This eventually led to resident doctors and a hospital. At that time the infant mortality rate here was the highest in Japan so we helped to tackle that problem first and we are glad to know that we have had a small share in lowering the rate.

In all of our work and life here we have tried to see the need and meet it as far as possible. This has led to a varied program different from most mission work.

Thomasine Allen

V. "The Way to Better Tomorrow"   215

(2) Dialogue between Two Fir Trees

In those days, in her reports, two fir trees appeared to carry
on a dialogue concerning Christmas activities. Two trees were
brought down from a mountain, and covered with Christmas
decorations. The big one stood up straight in the front of the
Center garden, but the small one was carried on the wagon
with Miss Allen and staff to the small rural villages, where
children and villagers were waiting impatiently.

[Report 23]

AGAIN THE TWO TREES

CHRISTMAS 1963

With prices going up and up, could we afford to have our
twenty Christmases this year, many of them in the byways
and hedges of this backward area? But on the other hand
could we afford *NOT* to them, and thus disappoint so many
children? And the answer of course was that even though
it meant going deeper into the hole we MUST take the
Christmas story and cheer to some of these neglected places.

So, on the 13th of Dec. the little portable tree climbed
into the jeep along with her decorations, flannel graph, a story
illustrated picture, literature, cards, candy etc. and started on
her travels which would take her many, many miles over hill
and dale. (Incidentally Mr. Yahaba and I went with her.) We
left at 8 o'clock going to a school 20 miles from here which
took two hours—even so, the roads were greatly improved—
and went immediately to the cold assembly room where 300

children were gathered. There seemed to be a slight haze but surely not smoke for there was no stove in sight—oh, it was the breath of the children. They were sitting quietly on the floor—some of them had brought little one-foot square 'cushions' about one inch in thickness, to sit on but I could not see what good they did, for they could not make the floor less hard, or the cold floor less cold. But those little children sat there for over three hours! Before the program some of the teachers and children helped to decorate me and I was proud to show my beauty to so many waiting children.

Miss Allen with the flannel graph told the story of the first Christmas and then all sang Silent Night. (This song is nationally known as it is in the school text books, and the radio blares out it all for days in stores, night clubs, bars and every place but how very few know what it is about or have any idea of the meaning.) Then Mr. Yahaba with the picture theater told the story of Why the Chimes Rang and the story of Zacchaeus (LUKE 19:1-10.flv). The baby Jesus became a man and the story of Zacchaeus showed part of his work. This story means much to Mr. Yahaba as when he was a H.S. student he stopped into a secondhand book store and picked up a book which happened to be the Bible. When he opened it the first thing he read was the story of Zacchaeus and he was deeply impressed.

If contact with Jesus could change a man so completely, and also his family, then he wanted to know more about Christianity—and that was the beginning of a new life for him. They followed the school's part of the program as each class wanted to do something for the occasion. It was then one o'clock, but no time for lunch as 30 women were waiting in one of the classrooms (where there was a stove) and we

V. "The Way to Better Tomorrow"   217

had an hour's meeting with them.

It was long after dark when we reached home - to start out early the following morning for two more places, even harder of access. When you get off the main road, you are in trouble - ruts like ravines, clay in which you get stuck and have to be pulled out, but we made it! And the black and blue spots do not count for these little mountain children have so little in their lives. As soon as they saw our jeep coming they immediately carried their desks and chairs out of the classroom, got buckets of water and cloths and began mopping the floor on hands and knees, built up the fire, helped to decorate me and then sat on the floor to enjoy the program.

Another event in the midst of the Little Tree's travels was the taking of warm Christmas cheer in the form of 66 futon (Japanese bedding) to 33 families in two fishing villages who had lost everything. We loaded our truck with the bright colored futon and started to the first village only to find that a short tunnel we must needs go thru was completely blocked by a cave-in, so there was nothing to do but turn around and go back but to turn on a narrow road with the sea far below you on one side and high mountains above you on the other side made turning easier said than done. We were most thankful that we had not been in the tunnel when it collapsed a short time before. Back we went and started for the second village where they were awaiting us with open arms, literally. (Several days later when the tunnel had been cleared we retraced our steps and gave them their futon.)

The third of the special events was a Christian wedding in our Center. One of our kindergarten teachers, a Kuji girl we had trained and who had been with us several years was married and we had the wedding for her. It was the first time most of the guests had ever seen a Christian wedding and they were quite impressed, and happy over it.

The Little Tree said to the Big Tree, "I believe you are the most beautiful tree in all Japan. You have shed your beauty and light to all who have come to the Christian Center for the different programs, —the kindergarten one with 300 crowded in the room, sitting on the floor, our primary and junior high schools which gave, "Why the Chimes Rang", in such a worshipful way it brought tears to the eyes of many, and the Sunday School Christmas when after the lovely program how glad you were to see the children who had not missed a Sunday for one year, for two years, for five years, for seven years and for eleven and twelve years called to the front and honored—about forty of them." And the Big Tree answered, "We each have our place to serve and also you are small maybe you have done a bigger work for you braved the cold and the bad roads which were sometimes dangerous to take the Christmas story and cheer to far-away places, where the children would have been so disappointed if you had not gone in spite of all the extra difficulties this year. You have let loving service triumph over the waves and billows."

Thus ends the story of the two trees but *NOT* the work of the Christian Center.

For all the help you have given us during the year and especially the extra help at flood time we want to again

V. "The Way to Better Tomorrow" | 219

thank you—

In case some of you do not know, some friends in America have organized the Kuji Christian Center Foundation, Incorporated, and thru that it is our hope, prayer and faith that the work can grow and become a brighter light to shine in the darkness. Miss Mary Coxhead is Chairman of the Exec. Committee and her address is 1215 Holman Road, Oakland, Cal. 94610. In case you want any further information please write to her.

Thomasine Allen

CHAPTER 3

Supporters:
She Made Kuji Her Permanent Home

(1) Kuji Christian Center Foundation (KCCF) (1964)

In 1964, the Kuji Christian Center Foundation was established by women's clubs of the churches in Oakland, California, Portland, Oregon, and Franklin, Indiana. It was authorized legally by the US government as a nonprofit foundation. The Center was formally called the Kuji Christian Center and was supported vigorously by Women's clubs of churches and friends in the United States. It was also profitable for contributors that they could reduce their taxes. And Miss Allen was released from her hard work to write letters every day and night. She, herself, also contributed her savings and her mother's property to the foundation.

Here is a paper left in one of her file books about KCCF.

V. "The Way to Better Tomorrow" 221

[Document 13]
"Kuji Christian Center Foundation"
Chairperson of Homare Educational Foundation
Thomasine Allen

Seat:	Inc. 1215 Holman Road Oakland. California 94610
Chairperson:	Miss Mary Coxhead
Board of Directors:	Dr. Maxwell T. Powers, Mrs. Maxwell T. Powers,
	Mrs. Grace P. Herring, Mrs. Leslie L. Bennet,
	Mr. John Nicolson, Mrs. Maurice B Hodge
Ex- Officio:	Miss Thomasine Allen, Mr. Takeshi Yahaba
Consultants:	Mrs. Harlow Russell, Mrs. Robert Hemphill,
	Mrs. Henderson B. Herod, Mrs. Edwin Reischauer
Sponsors:	Col. & Mrs. Crowford J. Smith, Mrs. Frances McCutcheon,
	Mr. & Mrs. John Dar, Miss Lena Daugherty,
	Mrs. Herbert, Mr. Fillebrown, Mr. & Mrs. Ed Gibson,
	Mr. & Mrs. Howard Hannaford, Col. & Mrs. Russell Steinhour,
	Mrs. Harry Walker, Mr. & Mrs. R.D. Anderson,
	Dr. Gene Bartlette, Miss Georgene Bowen, Mrs. B. B. Braden,
	Mr. & Mrs. Walker Bauer, Mr. & Mrs. Harlow Russell,
	Mrs. Duncan Mackenzie, Miss M. Rogers

How she was relieved for having this foundation! Already she was 74 years old! "KCCF really encouraged us to continue our programs. We had confidence that we were not isolated, not forgotten but supported strongly", she said by herself.

In September 1966, Miss Mary Coxhead visited Kuji in order to survey the circumstances of the Center; facilities, institutions and activities. She went around everywhere with Miss Allen and joined all events. She especially enjoyed "Summer Christmas" held in the small village, which was covered with snow in winter. She was very impressed with all the activities and understood them.

[Document 14]

This paper must be written by Mrs. Hemphil (Bitty)

I have not known Miss Allen as long as many of you have. I met her only ten years ago when I heard her speak in Tokyo. But I felt at once that she was remarkable person. When I began to work on a book about her life I talked with her and I talked with friends who had known her for a long time— both America friends and Japanese friends. I learned that she has three great qualities.

One is vision. She looked ahead and saw a church and a school long before they became realities. In the midst of suffering she looked ahead and saw deliverance.

One is common sense. She was willing to work long and hard and do the practical things necessary to make the visions reality.

The last is the gift of communication. Thousands of English speaking people came to love and understand Japan better with her help. Through this gift, all of us who have gathered here today have come to share her vision of better world and committed to work for its realization.

(2) *A Treasure to Share* was published.

Mrs. Elizabeth A. Hemphill lived in Japan from 1959 for several years, as a wife of a United States Air Force colonel and military counselor. She became personally acquainted with the work of Miss Allen. Soon she visited Miss Allen in Kuji and talked with her about her true experiences, recording on tape and taking notes. Mrs. Hemphill wrote the manuscript of *A Treasure to Share* in connection with her thesis for a master's degree from the department of religion at George Washington

V. "The Way to Better Tomorrow" | 223

University. As her principal source, she used actual tape recordings of Miss Allen and The Christians of Kuji.

"The JADSON PRESS" published 20,000 copies of *A Treasure to Share*. American people were greatly touched by this story. Mr. Blanche M. Hodge, a member of K.C.C.F., wrote the dedication FORWORD.

Mr. & Mrs. Hemphill also, as the members of KCCF, supported Miss Allen, and took much collection. Both of them became best friends, so Miss Allen chose her as an executor of her last will and testament.

[Document 15]

FOREWORD of *A Treasure to Share*

BLANCHE MOORE HODGE

NOW IT MUST BE TOLD!

It is the story of a pioneer missionary in Northern Japan. Like all trail blazers, Miss Thomasine Allen (known far and wide as "Tommy") has followed a vision leading her through unbelievable struggle filled with tears and heartbreak. Not only has she served as an American Baptist missionary in her beloved Japan for over forty years, but she has opened up a great new mission field.

She went out to Japan as a teacher in one of our denominational schools, but the underprivileged children in Iwate Ken on the coast and in the mountain areas of the north called to her. With straw mats under the trees she began Vacation Bible Schools—and then the dream for a kindergarten and mission began to take form. Always the needs of a growing, challenging work have been far greater than the resources.

Her story is one of joy and pathos, laughter and tears. Throughout it all the winsome personality and deep faith of Thomasine Allen shine forth. God has used a life to bring thousands of children and young people to know him and to find abundant life. Kuji, at the end of the railroad, and Tommy are synonymous.

(3) Dr. & Mrs. Edwin O. Reischauer visit Miss Allen

One of the readers of this book was American Ambassador to Japan and his wife, Mr. & Mrs. Edwin O. Reischauer. Mrs. Haru Reischauer, a daughter of Mr. Matsukata, had known Miss Allen for a long time before the WW II. The Matsukatas supported Miss Allen for her work in the isolated rural small town in Iwate.

On September 19 1965, Mr.& Mrs. E. O. Reischauer flew to Kuji from Misawa Air Base by helicopter and landed directly on the shores of the Osanai river just near Kuji Kindergarten. Miss Allen was overjoyed to hear his comments; "The children' eyes are brilliant. You taught them true love."

[Document 16]
Letter from Dr. E. O. Reischauer

Tokyo, August 4, 1964

Dear Miss Allen:

I just wanted to tell you that Haru and I have just

finished reading Mrs. Hemphill's excellent book on you and your work, "A Treasure to Share." Her husband has recently joined the Embassy staff as Military Attaché, and she was kind enough to give me a copy of her work. It is really an outstanding book, but then the subject deserves nothing but the best.

Haru keeps urging me to save time for a trip to see your work in Kuji. We certainly would like to do this, but I do not know when we can, because there are still so many ken capitals and big centers we haven't visited yet. However, we hope to get to Kuji some time.

Haru joins me in sending you our respects and best wishes.

Sincerely,
Edwin O. Reischauer

Miss Thomasine Allen,
Kuji, Iwate-Ken.

[Document 17]

Letter from Mrs. Haru Reischauer

Dear Miss Allen,

I just want to add a little note to my husband's to say how much we enjoyed

Mrs. Hemphill's book almost you and the Yahabas and Kuji.

You haven't been very good letting us know when you were coming to Tokyo. Please be sure to let us know next time you come. Ed and I will love to see you—I haven't seen you in years.

(4) Miss Allen's 50th Anniversary of Work in Japan

In 1965 the 50th anniversary of Miss Allen's work in Japan was celebrated by friends from all over Japan, and later by the city of Kuji. (106)

[Document 18]

EMBASSY OF THE
UNITED STATES OF AMERICA

Tokyo, October 1, 1965.

Dear Miss Allen,

Mrs. Reischauer and I would like to join with the people of Kuji and Iwate Ken and your friends throughout the world in offering congratulations to you on the anniversary of your fiftieth year in Japan.

You have been a fine representative in Japan of the best in American culture and an interpreter of Japanese culture in the United States. Your work in Kuji is well-known to those joining in this celebration. Less well-known is your work in the United States. When on home leave you have spoken to thousands of people in churches throughout America, broadening their understanding of Japan. You made a particular contribution in the years 1944-1945, when you travelled throughout the United States speaking sympathetically about wartime Japan, in a sometimes hostile atmosphere. The present state of cordial relations existing between our two countries is due in no small part to the work of persons like you.

V. "The Way to Better Tomorrow" | 227

Your concern for ethical and moral values and your long years of selfless service have won the admiration of both Japan and America. As a citizen of the United States and as an honorary citizen of Kuji-shi, you are one of person of whom both our countries can be proud.

Mrs. Reischauer and I had long cherished the hope of visiting you at the Kuji Christian Center, and we were extremely happy to be finally able to do so in September. We recall with pleasure the warm reception we received on that occasion, and we are delighted to be able through this letter to join with the citizens of Kuji and of Iwate Ken in congratulating you on the fiftieth anniversary of your arrival in Japan and to wish you continued success.

Sincerely,
Edwin O. Reischauer

Miss Thomasine Allen,
Kuji Christian Center,
Kuji, Iwate Ken, Japan.

[Document 19]

Omi-Hachiman,
Oct. 4, 1965

Dear Miss Allen:

Just I received an invitation to the grand celebration of your fifty years of service for Christ in Japan. And I learned that your service of Thirty-Two consecutive years in Kuji has brought to you honors most deserving of your merit.

I wish my time and strength were fit to bring myself to Kuji to witness your achievement, and to congratulate you in person. I have to preserve my aging strength for my service in Omi for the few remaining years on the earth. I regret very much that I am not able to come.

I have known of you these many years through my husband and Mr. and Mrs. Anderson of Oakland, California, who visited you and admired your work very highly. And I came to learn of your work by the personal contacts with Mr. Yahaba. He is one of your best achievements, I believe. You have reared in him the faith and character that will carry on your work into posterity.

I heartily congratulate you on your fiftieth year of service for the Kingdom of God. May God bless you and give you many more years of useful service in the happy circle of your co-workers.

Very sincerely yours,
Maki Vories Hitotsuyanagi

[Report 24]
THE DIALOGUE ON A HILLSIDE
1967 Christmas

Before the word 'dialogue' became so popular our two trees used that vehicle to describe the many Christmases of the various pieces of work carried on by the Kuji Christian Center.

A large fir tree and close by a small fir tree were talking on the hillside. "I think that surely we will be chosen this year to help tell the story of the Christ-Child," said the older tree. "But with all the heart-break, sorrow and suffering in the whole world I wonder if they will use us this year and if so, what can we do to alleviate the pain and give new hope, courage and love?" "You are big and beautiful and many

V. "The Way to Better Tomorrow"

adults as well as children hear the story thru you, but I am small, and besides it is largely children who see me, but; I do want to help—what can I do? "The Big Tree thought a minute and then said, "You can do what I do, both of us can give our lives. But till then we have a duty to perform, namely to let our twinkling lights shine in the darkness with a prayer that that will be symbolical of the coming of the Light to those who sit in darkness, and do not forget that it is a little child that shall lead them." And so it came to pass.

The two trees went joyfully to the Center where the Big Tree shone in splendor for the many Christmases there, all so beautiful, worshipful and inspiring—the Kindergarten, the School, the Young People, the Sunday School, the Church and finally the Staff. The Sunday school gave certificates for perfect attendance. Many received one for not missing a single Sunday for a year; some for five years, six, seven and eight years, and two for eleven and twelve years! That drew much applause and the Fig Tree smiled with pleasure.

The Little Tree did not complain when her branches were tied up and she was put into the jeep with boxes and boxes of decorations, cards, songs, flannelgraph, pictures stories and hundreds of bags of candy. This year to some of the smaller groups we gave bright, warm, colorful mittens from friends in America, and to certain groups, an unusual treat, a large hand-dressed American doll, likewise from American friends. Many were the ohs and ahs upon holding this treasure. The Little Tree was so excited over her first experience in this small isolated mountain school of 37 pupils she hated to leave, but another school was awaiting us so off with the decorations and on with the hurried packing and loading the jeep again. And we were soon bumping along the road to another isolated school where a welcome was awaiting us, and the Little Tree was again decorated.

Have you ever tried to give a flannel graph story with no place to put the board (two held it) and no place to put the figures and backgrounds plus having the children practically under your feet—one hundred packed in a small room? Well, it can be done and I have become an expert! There are always one or two places where this has to be done. Sometimes these country programs are held in schools, sometimes in village meeting rooms, and sometimes in private homes.

The climax of our whole Christmas season was on the afternoon of the 24th when Mr. Yahaba baptized ten people in the river. It was the most impressive and never-to-be-forgotten experience. Four H.S. students, one graduate, two 6th graders, two teachers and one kindergarten mother were baptized. After this we returned to our chapel for the Communion service—a fitting close to a full rich day.

The Big Tree said to the Little Tree when all the many programs were over and all had departed. "We were happy on the hillside when all we had to do was to grow, but we were happier still when we were chosen to give our lives to help in spreading the Good News of the coming of the Christ Child." And the Little Tree nodded assent.

Thomasine Allen

Kuji, Iwate Ken, Japan

(5) The Fourth Order of the Sacred Treasure

On October 23 1968, commemorating the Meiji Centennial, the Emperor honored Miss Allen with an Imperial Decoration, The Fourth Order of the Sacred Treasure. She was invited to the award ceremony at the Imperial Palace with sixteen foreign prize winners.

[Report 25] memo
In the dining hall a five-course luncheon was served after the Minister of Education had given a speech of congratulation to us. During the luncheon we were each asked to give an after-dinner speech. As the oldest and sitting next to the Minister of Education, I had to give the first.

The decoration is a sunburst of gold and rubies, very beautiful. The citation had been translated into English and a copy given to each of us along with the speech by the Minister of Education. I will quote here:

CONGRATULATORY SPEECH

BY THE MINISTER OF EDUCATION AT THE CEREMONY OF
TRANMITTING THE DECORATIONS TO THE FOREIGNERS

"It is my great honor to have been able to transmit to you the decorations which His Majesty the Emperor of Japan, in commemorating the Meiji Centennial, conferred upon you for the distinguished services you have made for many years for the development of education, science and culture in this country.

It is now one hundred years ago that the name of the era was changed from Keio to Meiji. In the Meiji Era we made a start to build a modern state. For these hundred years, we, Japanese, did not travel always a broad-level highway at all. In early days of Meiji, a drastic innovation of various systems and introduction of the western civilization into this country were made. It provided a solid foundation of the politics, education and industry of this country, to which owes much of what we have achieved in the present Japan as a modern state. Japan is now expected to assume a greater responsibility in the ever changing international community.

Such a remarkable growth and development of this country was made possible, by the development of education, science and culture to which you made a great help and contribution. I would like now, to pay my high tribute to express my sincere appreciation for the great efforts you made for us.

I hope that you will continue to help us in the further development of education, science and culture of this country.

In our group of sixteen I was the only one from the country side—all the others were from big cities and well-known schools and colleges and universities, so I felt the honor awarded me was really to this work of which Mr. and Mrs. Yahaba were co-founders and are co-workers.

It may seem a far cry from Christmas tree decorations to an Imperial Decoration, but the link which binds the two is

V. "The Way to Better Tomorrow" | 233

the Kuji Christian Center. The work that the trees symbolize, the bringing of the Light to the dark places in every phase of life have been recognized, honored, and appreciated by the Japanese Government. Many of you have made this possible thru your generous gifts, encouragement, and prayers, without which there would be no Kuji Christian Center.

> Thomasine Allen
> Kuji, Iwate Ken
> Japan

[Document 20]
CONGRATULATORY SPEECH

BY THE MINISTER OF EDUCATION
AT LUNCHEON
GIVEN IN HONOR OF THE FOREIGNERS WHO HAVE BEEN DECORATED
FOR DISTINGUISHED SERVICES

Ladies and Gentlemen,

I extend my sincere congratulation to all of you who have been decorated for your distinguished services in this country.

For many years, you have been living with us, Japanese, and making an outstanding contribution to the social and cultural development of this country.

I am very happy to see you having been awarded the decorations in this momentous year, 1968, in which we commemorate the Meiji Centennial.

You must have experienced not the least difficulties in living and working in a strange land. I would like to pay my high tribute to the unremitting efforts you made for us.

In closing, let me wish you a good health and the further prosperity or your work.

Michita Sakata
MINISTER OF EDUCATION

(6) What is Better for Higher Education:
High School or College?

Before this Prize, the Union of Japanese Private Kindergarten made a public recognition of the services rendered by Miss Allen as a long time employee. Her philosophy of education and contribution to northern Iwate were evaluated one after another. It occurred to the people that they should establish a school of higher education.

Iwate prefecture had a lot of land, but there were no universities or colleges in the wide northern area. Mr. & Mrs. Yahaba and other cooperators supported the plan of higher education in Kuji.

Since 1964, the board of directors of Homare Foundation had discussed this plan. In 1965, when Miss Allen went back to the United States, she consulted about this problem with members of KCCF.

In 1968, Miss Coxhead again visited Kuji. She reported that the Kuji Christian Center was going well, and 90% of graduates from middle school went on to high schools and colleges. The Dairy School was a big success with the neighboring farmers.

Miss Coxhead and KCCF suggested building a high school which had two courses; mechanics and general arts.

V. "The Way to Better Tomorrow" | 235

That would be good to bring a greater development to the Homare Foundation.

On Feb. 17, 1969, Mrs. Kuni Obara Yahaba died suddenly, while traveling in Hokkaido. She was the only one friend who could speak English! For forty years Kuni was her right hand! How Miss Allen grieved over the loss of her!

[Document 21]

Mrs. Edwin O. Reischauer
863 Concord Ave.
Belmont, Massachusetts 02178

February 28th

Dear Miss Allen,

Our thoughts are with you often, but today more so than usual, as we have heard about the loss of your devoted co-worker, Mrs. Yahaba. We send you our heartfelt sympathy. You have been blessed with such devout and dedicated friends at Kuji and we both feel great admiration for the Yahabas. We know that Mr. Yahaba is a tower of strength and so, despite this great loss, he will continue to carry on the great work they both devoted their lives to. We pray that progress will continue at Kuji.

We both want to congratulate you on your Imperial decoration for the second time. You of all Americans deserve this great honor.

We are now happily settled in Belmont—about fifteen minutes from Harvard. As of now we are surrounded by more than three feet of snow, having had two of the worst storms we have ever had. It is beautiful, but it will be lovely when it gets warmer.

We hope you will come see us if you should come this way. We have plenty of rooms for you to stay with us. Ed joins me in sending you deepest sympathy.

Affectionately,
Haru

In 1969, Mr. Yasuzo Shimizu, the President of Obirin University in Tokyo, visited Kuji and gave a lecture at the Center. He got a strong impression from Miss Allen and her works, so he recommended her to establish a college. He said, "higher education should bring great waves to the future in this country. You could educate the young peoples' souls, minds, and spirits. I'll help you to write papers to submit to the Ministry of Education. After a two-year course, if the students want to study more, they can transfer to our university."

His words were well grounded on actual fact. The percentage of students who went on to a higher stage of education in the areas was very low. The reason why Miss Allen decided to open a college in Kuji was not only for the brilliant futures of the young students but the energizing of these areas. The construction of buildings would give life to the towns, although there were high walls of funds to fly over. She wrote to Miss Coxhead about this plan and asked for support financially. In those days the United States was at war in Vietnam, so the market was not good, but Japanese business was very active.

Both ladies promised each other to pray together with the

prayer HABAKKUK 2:2 in two separate places; in Kuji and in America.

> *I will look to see what He will say to me. . . .*
> *Then the Lord replied: "write down the revelation*
> *and make it plain on tablets so that a herald may run with it.*
> *For the revelation awaits an appointed time;*
> *It speaks of the end and will not prove false.*
> *Though it liner, wait for it;*
> *It will certain come and will not delay.*
> *See, he is puffed up; His desires are not upright—*
> *But the righteous will live by his faith—*

As soon as they decided to found a college, they all started very hard works. It was sure that the financial aspect was the most difficult problem that confronted them. As a rough estimate, the cost would be more than $200,000. This vast sum of money was contributed by a lot of people from both America and Japan in order to educate Japanese young people in the isolated countryside.

[Report 26]
   The Little Tree Presents Her Problem

When the two trees entered the Kuji Christian Center, they felt something was lacking for there was a subdued atmosphere of sorrowing yet rejoicing. And the reason why? The Master Hand of Kuni who had planned all the Christmases for thirty years was not there. How-be-it her years of training

others now bore good fruit for all carried on in the beautiful
way she would have wanted.

As you know, the Big Tree always presided over the
various Kuji programs and the Little Tree over the country
ones, but this year TIME was a real problem, so we consulted
the two trees. The Big Tree said that she would gladly shine
overtime if we could do all the Kuji Christmases first. The
Little Tree said she didn't want to disappoint the children in
the rural schools so she thought she could make the travels
after the eight Kuji ones were over. And thus it came to pass.

And why was the time element so different this year?
Many of you know if you are in touch with our Kuji Christian
Center Foundation Inc. in Oakland, Cal. that we applied
to the National Ministry of Education to open a Junior
College as a further step in our work to make this dark place
a Center of Light. Last summer we studied the qualifications
for becoming accredited as a junior college and it seemed
absolutely impossible, but Japan was rapidly changing and
higher education was coming to the front so we should be
in a place of leadership, especially as there were only three
colleges in all of this big prefecture and none specializing
in English as we plan to do. But would Tokyo ever consent
to put a college in a country area like this part of Iwate?
And then the Minister of Education made a speech urging
universities and colleges to get out of Tokyo and into the
country. As that coincided with what we thought we ought
to do, we decided to make the plunge. This is not the place
to go into all the trials, troubles and tribulations we had; the
two Yahaba brothers doing the work of five men in preparing

V. "The Way to Better Tomorrow"

all the documents which it took four people to carry, the need of 5000 books books and ending up with 20,000 all catalogued and put in modern cases for our English library; Mr. Yahaba travelling all over Japan to get a faculty pleasing to the Educational Department; the necessity of starting at once on a reinforced concrete building as a first unit—to say nothing of a search for money—Big Money. And then at the last the arrival of two inspection teams a few days apart. Those were tense days. Of course all were noncommittal but we had reason to feel encouraged—but to wait for the final verdict was nerve-racking to say the least. It came Dec. 19th by radio, television and newspaper. We were one of four to receive this and the first one read out—and the only one in Japan to be located in the country off the main railroad line. It is quite an honor to Iwate Prefecture. Telegrams and letters of congratulations began coming this and fast—from many groups or people—State Legislature, State educational officials, principals of other schools, friends, former teachers and pupils and one from a Japanese doctor who had been on a ship with Kuni and me 42 years ago.

After the announcement was made we had lighter hearts but much more work to do!

We had promised to help the Big Tree so began with the costuming of the little children in "When The Littlest Camel (Knelt) and Holy Night", but I almost got lost in memories—here was a small shepherd with a short plaid jacket—the lining of a coat I had when I first came to Japan in 1915. Wise Men used lovely silk scarves bought in Cairo in 1927, their robes of red, blue and purple decorated with gold and silver paper were made by one of our summer schools in the 1930s when we held a summer Christmas pageant. And oh, yes, here on the littlest camel was my steamer rug which I had on my first voyage in 1915 on the Mongolia which had the distinction of carrying about 250 missionaries and returning ones many influenced by the goal proclaimed by Dr. John Moffit, "To evangelize the world in this generation." But I must quit thinking of the past and tend to the piano which seemed to have keys of ice not ivory.

Days later the Little Tree says, "Now it is my turn". So loading up we are off to two country places over roads which are gradually improving. The children were awaiting us looking forward to the trimming of the tree, the stories, songs and cards and candy—then taking off the decorations, packing up and going to the next place, after a cup of tea with the Principal and his wife who live in the building. Here as in other places, the smaller children received mittens and knitted caps—so they were most happy, Then another isolated school with a 'rice ball' supper eaten by us en route. Here we had the children first and afterwards the young people and parents.

In all of the gatherings we told them of the opportunity their children will have to attend junior college as it would be in the financial reach of all. We tried to explain to the teachers and student's parents the connection between the Little Tree shedding its light and the new school whose light can go much farther—even to Asia.

Later the two trees were heard talking together "We are a part of a bigger plan than we thought for some of these children will go on to our new college and then maybe as teachers or workers to different parts of Japan and Asia. It is our part to help train them." We want to join in giving

V. "The Way to Better Tomorrow" 241

thanks for cards, candy, which Misawa Air Base kindly brought over, mittens, caps—and everything so lovingly made and sent.

> For God will light our candle.
> Thomasine Allen

CHAPTER 4

Allen Junior College: Department of English Language and English Literature

On January 21, 1970, the Ministry of Education authorized the Homare Educational Foundation and approved the establishment of Allen Junior College. That was the moment when her dream came steadily true.

On April 21 at the new college building, the opening and the entrance ceremony was held with four new students and more than one hundred persons attending.

[Report 27]

OUR NEW JUNIOR COLLEGE

April 21, 1970

Have you ever seen the walls of Jericho come tumbling down and not just sung the words? Some of us have had that experience recently. The walls being a $100,000 debt to be paid in a year and during that most unusual year we were to do what nearly everyone said was impossible, obtaining

V. "The Way to Better Tomorrow" | 243

accreditation from the Ministry of Education and opening a Junior College specializing in English, in a very backward place. To even mention all the difficulties involved would fill a book—but suffice it to say those walls was tumbling down.

The financial dead line was approaching and the debt was slowly moving downward, but too slowly. I was the one responsible—the word of a Christian. If I failed? A. small dedicated, praying and giving group got together in spirit— East Coast, West Coast and Kuji, with a course of faith promises for meditation and prayer every day, looking first to our own lives to see if the conditions were being met, and expecting what seemed the impossible—and the walls came tumbling down.

The great and near-great gathered on the third floor of the new building on the 21st of April in person or by telegram—all of which were read later in the program. The Governor could not be present but sent a long message of greetings. The Mayor cancelled everything to tell how proud he was for Kuji to have this honor, an honor he never dreamed of and he was glad to have this way of strengthening ties with America. Representatives of many organizations read messages of congratulations.

As principal I gave the opening words of welcome, using my name as something on which to hang my remarks! 'Education' to the Japanese ear means only 'book leading and the passing of exams.' To us it means so much more—what about the heart as well as the head, the spirit as well as the mind, the character training, the home education, etc.

I did not want my name used in the naming of the college but for the present I could not help it. However, I felt better when I thought I could make it a memorial, in my own mind at least, to my mother, Mrs. Allen, who 80 years ago dedicated her life to the education of two small children, putting the best of literature, art and music into the home with religious training. And my first name, Thomasine, especially could be used. It was practically the same pronunciation as the Japanese word for 'soul' (when I first heard it in a sermon, I thought somebody must be calling me). And so the two names cover what we are trying to do.

At the close of the program we went to the 4th floor roof garden for pictures and then down to two class rooms for Japanese lunches. The next two or three years will be very hard financially —what pioneer work isn't? A child in America wrote me saying she heard I needed money for this work and enclosed a dollar bill. "Is this enough?" she asked. Of course I thanked her and wanted to say but didn't, "Yes, if you can put lots of zero after the 1."

The younger Mr. Yahaba had a dream—he was driving and overtook Kuni—he asked her to get in but she answered that she was turning at the next road but for him to go straight forward. "Go Straight Forward," she said, and that is what we are trying to do.

Thomasine Allen

[Note 3]

The Opening Address of Allen Junior College

V. "The Way to Better Tomorrow" | 245

One of my earliest introductions to Iwate ken was meeting Dr. Nitobe and having dinner with him in Sendai. Dr. Nitobe was one of Japans great statesmen and he could interpret his country to the world because of his command of the English Language.

Again as Japan leads this part of the world and takes her place of leadership in the U.N. "communication" is the key word—and that key is English.

To make Iwate stronger in higher education; to emphasize the need for English to better understand world problems; and to secure better positions for graduates we are opening the Junior College to specialize in English.

Thomasine Allen

[Note 4]
EDUCATIONAL PRINCIPLES

This school was founded with the intent of
a) Presenting broad-based academic and cultural knowledge in accordance with the "Fundamental Law of Education" and the "School Education Law",
b) Providing a place for a scientific and realistic approach to the study and teaching of special fields in the arts and sciences and
c) Providing an education grounded in the values of the Christian Faith.
In addition, this school seeks to raise citizens having an acquaintance with great ideas and practical language ability through the study of literature and language; that study being based on a broad, international perspective, a vital

inner force, a cultivated sense of sentiment, a love or peace
and freedom and a spirit of devoted service to society.

Thomasine Allen

Allen International Junior College had a good curriculum as a
department of English and English Literature, which above all
included several subjects for teacher-training courses and some
subjects for transfer examinations to the university. Excellent
professors came from other cities; Morioka, Sendai, Tokyo and
so on. Mr. Kiyosawa drove almost every day for more than 7
or 8 hours, to bring the professors to Kuji from Morioka or
Misawa airport. Miss Allen had many shadow collaborators
like him.

The college was a residential college so students gathered
from various places.

Training "ability of communication in English and human
dignity" to young people was the college's purpose. In the dormitory, through daily life, students would learn a lot about
ideas, manners, and how to communicate and debate. The
graduates wrote about Miss Allen in their reports.

"Miss Allen didn't talk much to us about her faith or Love
of God, but we could feel this by her dignified manner and
her way of speaking. Although she was very aged, she always
showed us her high spirituality."

"She was very gentle and quiet but in the class she was just
opposite. She never missed her classes even if she looked

V. "The Way to Better Tomorrow" | 247

not so well. We realized her serious attitude on 'pride and responsibility to work'."

"We begin to show a close resemblance to what we "see" through the heart and not through the eyes. We should look at everything through the heart."

[Report 28]
THE TWO TREES AGAIN WALK AND TALK
1970

"To go or not to go, that is the question", said the Little Tree as it watched the Big Tree being taken from its mountain home to decorate the Kuji Christian Center where many Christmas services were to be held.

The Little Tree heard the men from the Center talking, saying, "What can we do this year? With more groups in Kuji and more work to be done in connection with them so that they would convey thru the beauty of worship the real spirit of Christmas, we cannot possibly take all of the country trips too. Besides this, in order to save money some of the staff was planning to make cup cakes and cookies (about 2000) instead of buying candy. This would take much time day and night, but the more they thought about it the more they knew they could not omit all the country places, so selected about five of the smallest and most isolated groups". And so it thus came to pass, and the Little Tree was made happy by being taken along with the Big Tree to play its lowly part, shining bravely for the children who were awaiting its coming.

BUILD UP, BUILD UP, PREPARE THE ROAD!

The opening of new work in Kuji added much work to our full program. The highest point was the baptism of six in the early afternoon of the 24th, in the river! One of our new college students went to Mr. Yahaba a few weeks before Christmas and said he wanted to be baptized at Christmas time. He said that he had not seen a Bible nor knew what Christmas was till he came to Kuji last April. Someway he felt there was a great difference in atmosphere and living and realized the difference was Christianity. The change in him was sudden and complete—he became a much better student, a happier and kinder person—born again. "I am so happy every day", he said, "and I want to go home and tell my friends about this school and the happy life of Christians". The others baptized were teachers, students, and towns' people. After the baptism—a very impressive service—we returned to the chapel room in the Center building for the Communion service. That night this new group of Christians and many more of our number went caroling—ending a rich full day. The day must be remembered.

The Big Tree so beautiful in her decorations proudly presided over the many services and programs of the many groups and departments of our work. At the close of the Church School honorable mention was made of children who had not missed a Sunday for a year, two years, five etc. And there were two who had not missed for 15 years! These two are in Tokyo now but attend Church School just the same.

The Little Tree was anxious to get started on her rounds

V. *"The Way to Better Tomorrow"* | 249

of five country places. Three of our staff and two of our newly baptized Christians packed the jeep with the important tree, decorations, cards, pictures, mittens etc. and started off to a little school of twenty-five students far away in the mountains. A man and his wife live in the school and are the faculty. The children lost no time when they saw us coming, getting the room ready, building a big fire in the stove, carrying in wood, and helping to set up the tree and decorate it. Mothers came too and enjoyed our program as we were an "all-star cast." The children remembered the Christmas songs we had taught them and enjoyed singing them. Then we taught more songs, several Christmas stories by pictures and the giving out of cards and mittens. We had the mothers remain and gave them several boxes of warm clothing to divide among the neediest in the mountain district, (the conditions are somewhat better these days.) Before going to the next place we sat around the stove and ate our rice balls and drank tea, and talked to the teachers.

The next place on our itinerary for that day was a village assembly room—also far away. Unlike the school no one seemed to be in charge and it was dirty and cold—no fire at all. We could clean up the worst places but did not feel free to make a fire in the stove, as we were guests. How does one get used to freezing?? The children had on lots of clothes and did not seem to mind the cold but it took me a long time to get thawed out when we got home late in the evening.

The two trees were happy that they could be used to bring loving cheer to so many people and hope with us that the knowledge of Christmas and its true spirit maybe wider and deeper as the years go by.

Thomasine Allen
Takeshi Yahaba
Kuji, IwateKen, Japan.

VI

"Dwell Deep"

CHAPTER I

In Her Later Years

Miss Allen spent her later days as the chairperson of the Homare Educational Foundation and principal of Allen Junior College. What was she thinking and how was she worried about the happier life of villagers? Did she think the same as when she heard God's message in her young days? "I want to work through you in that isolated, difficult place, and I will show you the way to soften the soil. It must be by *blood of sacrifice, sweat of physical and spiritual labor, and tears of heartbreak*, discouragement, and disappointment."

Yes! She had never changed her ways of thinking.

"I am needed to help to carry the financial load. I must live to get this place self-supporting—or anyway, so I think!" But she had no illusions now about what "this generation" could accomplish; instead she had an abiding faith in what God could do and had done.

VI. "Dwell Deep"

[Report 29]

THE LITTLE TREE IS HAPPY

Kuji, Iwate Ken, Japan

Christmas 1973

And why is she happy? Because it is time for her to make her country travels which former Little Trees have told her about so delightfully.

The Big Tree, set up in the Kuji Christian Center all lighted and decorated, proudly displaying her beauty for all to see, opened the Christmas Season with the kindergarten celebration, to the delight of a room full of parents and children, on the 19th. From then on, there were one or two programs every day, either at the Center or in the country, till the 27th.

The Little tree never complained once when her branches were tied and she was put in the Jeep with boxes of decorations and cards and driven over icy roads many miles, sometimes to a school, sometimes to a big farmhouse, or the village hall, to be untied, set up and decorated by happy children. Then the lusty singing of Christmas songs which older children remembered from former years and younger children were taught. Then came the telling of the Nativity story by pictures, other Christmas stories, the giving out of cards, tying up the Little Tree again and then off to the next place, eating our luncheon of rice balls en route.

This year was marked by two separate advances which made it memorable. Four of our younger Christian teachers wanted to help, so we had them teach the songs and sometimes tell the stories so they can take charge if for any reason Mr. Yahaba or I cannot go. Also, one teacher was so interested that he opened his house for a neighborhood Christmas in Kuji.

In October, eight students had signified their desire to become Christians and were being instructed. Two of the eight were ready for baptism and asked to have it on the 24th of December in the river. I suggested waiting till spring, but they wanted it at the Christmas season, as that means something special to them. The Church folk met in the Center Chapel at noon and listened to the confession of faith of the two (a boy and a girl) then all gathered at the river, where a big fire had been built and tents put up. It was an impressive ceremony. Then we returned to the Center Chapel for the Lord's Supper and to welcome the new members into the fellowship of the church.

This lasted till five o'clock and then at 6:30 we met again for our traditional Candle Light Service. All was dark, till one by one over fifty came in slowly, while I played Largo, and lighted his or her candle at the central Light on the altar, then stood in the general form of a cross while Bible passages were read and hymns sung depicting the Light Giving work of Jesus, closing victoriously in "Joy to the World", with all lights gleaming.

And thus we enter 1974—

Thomasine Allen

[Report 30]
THE LITTLE TREE IS COLD
Christmas 1974

"This the first time I have envied you", said the Little Tree to the Big One as both were brought in from the mountain

VI. "Dwell Deep"   255

and put in the Christian Center building to prepare them for their life of giving light and beauty to many who would have no Christmas celebration if it were not for them.

"Little Tree, you are not complaining, aren't I?" "No, I am not complaining, I am just cold from my topmost branch to my roots." "Let me tell you something that will warm your heart as it did mine". Miss Allen received many letters from all over America and even from Germany asking about us and wondering if we were going on our Christmas mission of taking the story of the Christ Child to children living in faraway places who have no Sunday school or church to tell them the Bible stories we know and love. In one American Sunday School, the little third grade children did various kinds of work for which they earned some money—then brought it to Sunday school to give the teacher, tell how it was earned and ask that it be sent to Kuji for the Christmas programs where Miss Allen takes the trees to places around Kuji. Aren't you glad you have been chosen to take the Christmas story to twelve different places where they are anxiously waiting for your coming?" "Well, that is a lovely story—thank you for telling me, for that will help me bear having my branches tied up and being jolted over bumpy roads and being cold!"

The children see us coming, hasten to put more wood in the stove, for we look cold, help to take the things out of the Jeep, decorate the tree and then sing their Christmas songs which they remember from the last year. In the main our program consists of telling the story of the birth of the Christ Child using the flannel-graph and interspersing the story with songs; telling a story showing the Christmas spirit, and closing with slides of 'The Other Wise Wan'. Then some little bags of candy are given to each with a Christmas card. After the closing song, the children help to disrobe the tree and take it and the other things out to the Jeep. Then we are off to the next place, eating our rice balls on the way.

This year, these programs were sometimes given in a country school, in the village hall or in a home. If a home, the family and neighbors were invited in. The adults stayed long after the children had gone and enjoyed the talk over the tea cups sitting around the charcoal fire which looked warm, but which heat did not reach very far. But, this is an important time of these Christmases and sometimes lasts till almost midnight—then home again for more programs the next day.

The programs at the Center were exceptionally lovely this year—all the teachers putting forth every effort to make them worshipful. At the close, special honor was given to those who had not missed a Sunday for 3, 4, 5, 6 or even 7 years.

A Happy New Year to You All—

Thomasine Allen

T. Yahaba

Kuji, Iwate Ken, Japan

Please share with the Caravan Group who came to Kuji. Do come again.

We appreciate yours (?) in touch. Prayers.

Lovingly T. Allen

CHAPTER 2

On Her Deathbed

Listening to the sounds of children, through the halls of the kindergarten to the college, she used to drag one foot after another at a slow speed. It was such a pitiful scene. On February 9, 1976, from sudden gusts of cold wind she slipped and fell at the front of the kindergarten entrance. Immediately she was carried to the hospital next to the college. Her thighbone was broken, so she was hospitalized in Kuji City Hospital. Her long hospital life began. It was tragic that she could never return to her house. During these days she could not walk, not to mention move, so she aged very rapidly. She sometimes murmured by herself, "I want to go back! Where? To her house, to her mother?" "To God."

One of her best friends, Mrs. Cornelia L. R. Schroer, a professor of Iwate Junior college in Morioka, visited her in the hospital in Kuji and was so astonished to see her sorrowful figure, because on the bed she could not move or express herself in English and not enough in Japanese. She had both arms and legs tied to the bed like on a cross, and struggled to free by herself. Immediately Mrs. Schroer decided to move her to Morioka hospital, with the intention of nursing her in English. In spite of Mrs. Schroer's excellent care, Miss Allen breathed her last at 10:05 on June 7, while Mrs. Schroer had a class. She wrote "Miss Allen looked as if she were on a cross on her deathbed. At first I thought I had to thank God he had guided her to the land of the free."

The funeral service, held on June 23 in the small hall of Kuji Kindergarten by the Rev. Takeshi Yahaba, was attended by a lot of graduates and believers. The Kuji City held a Civic Funeral service for the Honorary Citizen, Miss Allen, where more than six hundred people attended from everywhere and offered heartfelt prayers and expressed their gratitude to her.

VI. "Dwell Deep"

My Prayer for You

This is my prayer,
that your love may abound more and more
in knowledge and depth of insight,
so that you may be able to discern what is best
and may be pure and blameless
for the day of Christ,
filled with the fruit of righteousness
that comes through Jesus Christ—
to the glory and praise of God.
(Phil. 1: 9-11, NIV)

Bibliography

Dewey, John. *Democracy and Education*. The Macmillan Company: N.Y., 1920.

吉田悦蔵・佐藤安太郎『近江の兄弟』湖畔堂出版部：滋賀県，1923.

Wynd, William. *Seventy Years in Japan: Saga of Northern Baptists*. The American Baptist Foreign Mission Society: New York, 1943.

日本聖書協会『聖書』Bible Coll. Japanese: 東京，1955.

International Bible Society. *The HOLY BIBLE*. Zondervan Publishing House: Michigan.

賀川豊彦全集刊行会『賀川豊彦全集』第8・9巻，キリスト新聞社：東京，1964.

Hemphill, Elizabeth. *A Treasure to Share*. Judson Press: Valley Forge, 1964.

百年史記念委員会『日本バプテスト宣教百年史』日本バプテスト同盟：東京，1973.

新渡戸稲造『農業本論』農文協：東京，1976.

内川永一朗『晩年の稲造』岩手日報社：盛岡，1983.

コーネリア・R．シュレーヤー『ひかりをかゝげた婦人たち』山口北州印刷：盛岡，1983.

大嶋晃一「岩手の廃娼運動」『岩手県立博物館研究報告書』第3号，71-96頁，盛岡，1985.

聖光幼稚園の歩み編集委員会『聖光幼稚園の歩み』（学）聖光学園：塩釜，1985.

Schroer, Cornelia R. & Gilbert W. *Through the Storm*. Sashimaya Printing Company: Aizu Wakamatsu City, 1991.

小檜山ルイ『アメリカ婦人宣教師』東京大学出版会：東京，1992.

角谷晋次『みちのくの三愛運動』キリスト新聞社：東京，1993.

米沢和一郎「新渡戸稲造と賀川豊彦」『新渡戸稲造研究』第 2
号，新渡戸稲造会：盛岡，1993.

澤野正幸・たまえ『たからを分かちて』アレン国際短期大学：久
慈，1995.

宍戸朗太『バプテスト派の初期伝道誌』耕風社：気仙沼，1995.

斎藤久吉『東北農村と福音』聖農学園の歴史刊行会：塩釜，
1997.

鳥居清治・内川永一朗『新渡戸稲造と協同組合運動』（財）新
渡戸基金：盛岡，1997.

無明舎出版編『新聞資料東北大凶作』無明舎出版：秋田，2001.

山下文男『昭和東北大凶作』無明舎出版：秋田，2001.

R. L. スティブンス『根づいた花』河内愛子訳，キリスト新聞社：
東京，2003.

Karl-Heinz Schell. *Kagawa Toyohiko Sein soziales und politisches
Wirken.* ［K.-H. シェル『賀川豊彦 ― その社会的・政治的活動』
後藤哲夫訳，教文館：東京，2009.］

（宗）久慈教会記念誌刊行会編『神は愛なり』久慈教会記念誌
刊行会：久慈，2010.

Afterword

In November 2002, both Homare Educational Foundation and Allen International Junior College were taken over by the Tohoku Bunka Gakuen University Educational Foundation in Sendai, and finally closed in 2007. Only Kuji Kindergarten around large linden trees shows the works done by Miss Allen. The fine building is expanded by the new Foundation and is well maintained so beautifully shining the same as seventy-five years ago.

There are so many graduates who studied under the educational principles of Miss Allen. They are actively working in various fields living not only in Japan but all over the world. Missing school days in the campus they sometimes visit Kuji, where they could hear the voice of Miss Allen still living within their hearts, they said. She has been respected as an honorable citizen of Kuji. Her fundamental principle "Happy life by helping each other" was well infiltrated into these rural areas with their own traditions. The people have been working very diligently. Dairy farming, agriculture and fishery have been successful with ingenious ideas. Social welfare is also well organized.

After experiencing the Great East Japan Earthquake and the

Disaster of the Fukushima Nuclear Plants, I believe each of us is being questioned on his or her own position in this country and also our country, itself, is being questioned on its fundamental principle. Although our future is not clear and unpredictable, we must have the courage to take a new step forward. Miss Allen is showing us "the road" we should take. I believe that Miss Allen's footsteps taken during her 86-year life and her noble ideas, will serve as a guide for Japan in the future.

As the last chairperson of Homare Educational Foundation, I worked until it was shut down. Furthermore, as the last president of Allen International Junior College, I saw the last graduates off. I had been thinking that I had to convey the history to all concerned about Miss Allen's life and her work. However, I'd spent several years without doing so. Finally this book has come to be published in Japanese in 2012. Here, I wrote it in English for expressing gratitude to the people who supported for Miss Allen and her works. I strongly hope many people to know that one American woman could not only spread "a real human life with love", but also achieve the modernization of life in a small town of northern area of Japan.

I am sincerely thankful to all the people who have helped and supported me.

Especially, I wish to express my gratitude to Mrs. Kazuko Sato who gave advice and courage to write this book in

English. I also am grateful to Mr. and Mrs. Mitsuhiro Inoue and Mr. and Mrs. Tatsuo Suzuki who gave me several words of guidance. I am grateful to Mr. Mitsuru Watabe, president of Kyobunkwan for publication of this book, and to Mr. Masato Takahashi of the department of publishing for editing it. Lastly, thanks to my husband and my three children, I could work in Kuji isolated from you for more than twenty-five years.

May 10, 2014
Yasuko MEGURO

《著者略歴》

目黒安子（めぐろ・やすこ）

1935 年，仙台市生まれ。宮城学院中学・高校卒業。58 年，東北大学文学部フランス文学科卒業。78 年より北海学園大学，岩手大学にて非常勤講師。82 年よりアレン短期大学（のちにアレン国際短期大学）に勤務。83 年，モンペリエ大学に短期留学。2005 年，アレン国際短期大学最後の卒業生を送り出して定年退職する。
　現在，鎌倉在住。

著書

『みちのくの道の先——タマシン・アレンの生涯』（教文館，2012 年）。

Build up, Build up, Prepare the Road!
——The Life of Miss Thomasine Allen

2015 年 3 月 31 日　初版発行

著　　者　目黒安子
発 行 者　渡部　満
発 行 所　株式会社　教文館
　　　　　〒104-0061 東京都中央区銀座 4-5-1
　　　　　電話 03(3561)5549　FAX 03(5250)5107
　　　　　URL http://www.kyobunkwan.co.jp/publishing/
印 刷 所　モリモト印刷株式会社

配 給 元　日キ版　〒162-0814 東京都新宿区新小川町 9-1
　　　　　　　　　電話 03(3260)5670　FAX 03(3260)5637

© 2015　Yasuko Meguro　　　　　　　　　　　Printed in Japan
ISBN 978-4-7642-9964-1　　落丁・乱丁本はお取替えいたします。